National 4 & 5

History

Migration and Empire 1830–1939

Claire Wood
Simon Wood

Series Editor: John A. Kerr

HODDER GIBSON
GIBSON
AN HACHETTE UK COMPANY

The Publishers would like to thank the following for permission to reproduce copyright material:

Photo credits: **p.1** www.scottishviewpoint.com; **p.4** The Granger Collection/TopFoto; **p.5** Topfoto; **p.6** National Museums Northern Ireland; **p.12** © Scottish Life Archive, National Museums of Scotland. Licensor www.scran.ac.uk; **p.19** UK City Images/TopFoto; **p.20** UK City Images/ TopFoto **p.21** © CSG CIC Glasgow Museums Collection; **p.22** Getty Images; **p.28** Glasgow City Archives and Special Collections; **p.29** HIP/TopFoto; **p.30** © Penicuik Historical Society. Licensor www.scran.ac.uk; **p.38** (top) ScotFoto.co.uk/TopFoto.co.uk, (bottom) Elizabeth Leyden/Alamy; **p.40** © reproduced with permission of Scottish Jewish Archives Centre; **p.42** Topham Picturepoint; **p.43** D.G.Farquhar/Alamy; **p.49** (top) © Scottish Life Archive, National Museums of Scotland. Licensor www.scran.ac.uk, (bottom) Scottish Life Archive, National Museums of Scotland; **p.51** Getty Images; **p.57** (left) Library and Archives Canada item C-095320, (right) Glenbow Archives Poster 21; **p.58** Reproduced by permission of the National Library of Scotland; **p.59** (top and bottom) © National Records of Scotland. Licensor www.scran.ac.uk; **p.69** Topham Picturepoint; **p.70** Image Asset Management Ltd./Alamy; **p.71** (top) The Granger Collection/TopFoto, (bottom) Supapics/Alamy; **p.77** University of North Texas Libraries, The Portal to Texas History, http://texashistory.unt.edu; **p.78** (top) Hulton-Deutsch Collection/Corbis, (bottom) The Granger Collection/TopFoto; **p.83** Mary Evans Picture Library/Pump Park Photography; **p.84** © National Maritime Museum, Greenwich, London; **p.89** (top) Bettmann/Corbis, (bottom) Dundee Heritage Trust: Verdant Works; **p.91** Classic Image/Alamy; **p.96** Broad, Alf Scott, 1854–1929, National Library of Australia, nla.pic-an8955120.

Every effort has been made to trace all copyright holders, but if any have been inadvertently overlooked the Publishers will be pleased to make the necessary arrangements at the first opportunity.

Although every effort has been made to ensure that website addresses are correct at time of going to press, Hodder Gibson cannot be held responsible for the content of any website mentioned in this book. It is sometimes possible to find a relocated web page by typing in the address of the home page for a website in the URL window of your browser.

Hachette UK's policy is to use papers that are natural, renewable and recyclable products and made from wood grown in sustainable forests. The logging and manufacturing processes are expected to conform to the environmental regulations of the country of origin.

Orders: please contact Bookpoint Ltd, 130 Park Drive, Abingdon, Oxon OX14 4SE. Telephone: (44) 01235 827720. Fax: (44) 01235 400454. Lines are open 9.00–5.00, Monday to Saturday, with a 24-hour message answering service. Visit our website at www.hoddereducation.co.uk. Hodder Gibson can be contacted direct on: Tel: 0141 848 1609; Fax: 0141 889 6315; email: hoddergibson@hodder.co.uk

© Claire Wood and Simon Wood 2013

First published in 2013 by
Hodder Gibson, an imprint of Hodder Education,
An Hachette UK Company
2a Christie Street
Paisley PA1 1NB

Impression number	5	4	3	2	
Year	2017	2016	2015	2014	

Cover photo © Paul Schutzer/Time & Life Pictures/Getty Images
Illustrations by Gray Publishing
Produced and typeset in 10/11pt Folio Light by Gray Publishing, Tunbridge Wells
Printed in Dubai

A catalogue record for this title is available from the British Library

ISBN: 978 1444 187 236

Contents

Preface

This is one of a series of six titles for the National 4 & 5 History courses to be assessed from 2014 onwards. Students should study three main units in National 4 & 5 History, with a very wide selection of topics to choose from (five in the first two, ten in the third). This series covers two topics in each unit.

The six titles in the series are:

▶ National 4 & 5 History: Migration and Empire 1830–1939
▶ National 4 & 5 History: The Era of the Great War 1910–1928
▶ National 4 & 5 History: The Atlantic Slave Trade 1770–1807
▶ National 4 & 5 History: Changing Britain 1760–1900
▶ National 4 & 5 History: Hitler and Nazi Germany 1919–1939
▶ National 4 & 5 History: Free at Last? Civil Rights in the USA 1918–1968

Each book will contain comprehensive coverage of the four areas of mandatory content for National 5 as well as guidance and practice on assignment writing and assessment procedures.

The Assignment: what you need to know

National 5

What is the Assignment for National 5?

The Assignment is an essay written under exam conditions and then sent to the SQA to be marked. It counts for 20 marks out of a total of 80, so doing well in the Assignment can provide you with a very useful launchpad for overall success in the National 5 exam.

What can I write about?

You can write about a question linked to this book or something from another section in the course. In fact, you can write about any historical topic you want. You can even do your Assignment on local history.

What should I write about?

If you decide to do an Assignment based on the content of this book, here are some *good* possible questions:

✓ How important were the Highland clearances in causing Scots to migrate?
✓ To what extent did immigrants make a positive impact on Scotland?
✓ How significant was the economic contribution of immigrants to the development of Scotland?
✓ To what extent did Scots contribute to the countries they settled in?
✓ 'Scots had a negative impact in the countries they settled in.' How valid is this view?

What follows are *bad* titles for an Assignment:

✗ Scottish people left because there were more opportunities abroad.
✗ Immigrants lived in different parts of Scotland.
✗ The Irish in Scotland.
✗ Empire and the Scots.
✗ Scots did bad things to native people in the countries they moved to.

Be safe! There are no prizes for giving yourself a difficult question that you have made up yourself.

Choose something from the history you have already been studying.

Avoid doing something risky – you only get one chance at this Assignment.

How long should my Assignment be?

Your Assignment has no set length – it is what you can write in 1 hour. Most essays are about four or five pages long.

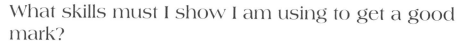

What skills must I show I am using to get a good mark?

▶ You must choose a question to write about. That means your title should end with a question mark. Don't just write a heading down because you will just start writing a story or a project. Your teacher is allowed to give you a little help with making your choice of title.

▶ Collect relevant evidence from *at least* two sources of information. For example, these could be two books or one book plus an interview.

▶ Organise and use your information to help answer your question.

▶ Use your own knowledge and understanding to answer the question that you have chosen.

▶ Include *at least* two different points of view about your question in your answer.

▶ Write a conclusion that sums up your information and ends up by answering the question you started with.

Remember that you also have a Resource Sheet to help you

On your Resource Sheet you will write out the sources that you will refer to in your essay. This will show the marker that you have researched, selected and organised your information.

Your Resource Sheet will be sent to the SQA with your finished essay. You will not be given a mark for your completed Resource Sheet but markers will use it to see that you have done the necessary research and have found appropriate sources to use in your Assignment. There is no time limit for completing your Resource Sheet and no word count. The Resource Sheet is *yours*. You can change it, colour it or print it out. You can write it anywhere, anytime before you write your Assignment under exam conditions.

National 4: Added Value Unit

The Assignment lets you show off your skills as you research a historical issue. You have a lot of choice in what you can find out about and you can also choose to present your findings in different ways. That means you don't have to write an essay to display your skills, knowledge and understanding.

To be successful in National 4 you have to show you can research and use information by doing the following things:

▶ Choosing an appropriate historical theme or event for study. Your teacher can help you choose.
▶ Collecting relevant evidence from *at least two* sources of information.
▶ Organising and using the information that you have collected to help you write about the subject you have chosen.
▶ Describing what your chosen subject is about.
▶ Explaining why your chosen subject happened (its cause) or explaining what happened next because of your chosen subject (its effects).

As you work through this book you will make mobiles, give presentations, and create posters and artwork. All these things could be part of your National 4 Assignment. You then have to present your findings.

Don't worry – if you get stuck your teacher is allowed to give you help and advice at *any* stage as you do your Assignment.

Do I have to write a long essay?

No, you don't. You can choose how you present your Assignment. You could do a talk and then be asked some questions about your subject by your teacher. You could do a PowerPoint presentation or keep a learning log or design a poster or some other way to display your work. You could even write an essay if you wanted to!

Chapter 1 Introduction

What is this course about?

The course is about why many Scots decided to move abroad between 1830 and 1939. It is also about why many people from different cultures and backgrounds came to live in Scotland during the same period. This book looks at the experiences that people had as a result of moving to new countries or communities. Finally, this book moves on to look at the effects, both good and bad, that Scots had on the British Empire and the effect the Empire had on Scottish society.

What will this book help me to do?

This book will help you to be successful in your National 5 and 4 History course. It contains everything you need to know about all the mandatory content and illustrative examples provided by the SQA for 'Migration and Empire 1830–1939'.

The book provides advice and examples to help you to answer all the different types of question you are likely to face in the National 5 exam.

Finally, this book will provide guidance to help you work on the Added Value Assignment tasks.

Homecoming year

Scotland hosted the first Homecoming year in 2009 and will repeat it in 2014.

▶ Who are coming 'home' and why?
▶ What connection is there to the old idea of the British Empire – and why?
▶ Why do so many Scots share a culture with a land outside Scotland?
▶ Why do so many people scattered around the world still think of Scotland as home?

The answers to these questions are what this book is really about.

Additional resources

Find out more about Scotland and what it is doing to connect migrants with the country:

▶ **www.visitscotland.com/see-do/homecoming-scotland-2014/**
▶ **www.ancestralscotland.com**
▶ **www.scotlandspeople.gov.uk**
▶ **www.cometoscotland.com**

Chapter 2   Who came to Scotland?

What is this chapter about?

Many different people travelled to Scotland in the years between 1830 and 1939. Some of these people stayed in Scotland and made it their home. This chapter explains why some Irish people made Scotland their home.

By the end of this chapter you should be able to:

▸ Describe the main immigrant groups that came to Scotland.
▸ Explain why and when Irish people came to Scotland.

Where did people who came to Scotland come from?

The main **immigrant** groups that came to Scotland were the Irish, Jewish, Italian and Lithuanian, Asian and English peoples. Jews, Italians and Lithuanians came mainly from eastern and southern Europe.

Why did Irish people come to Scotland?

At first, Irish people came to Scotland to work for the summer and then returned home to Ireland. Up until 1922, the whole of Ireland was part of the UK. This meant that Irish people were likely to come to Scotland because it was part of the same country. Another reason was the closeness of Ireland to Scotland. Look at the map on page 3. Irish people moved to Scotland because it would have been relatively cheap to do so.

Irish people came for seasonal jobs which earned them money to support their families back home. They came to help bring in the harvest and were known as reapers. They worked from the end of June to the end of October before most

> Look at the bar chart. When do you think Irish immigration was at its highest? Choose a piece of evidence from the bar chart that supports your answer.

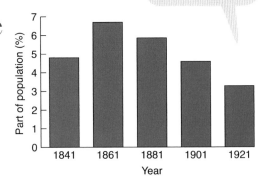

The number of Irish-born people living in Scotland.

GLOSSARY

Immigrant a person coming to live permanently in a different country

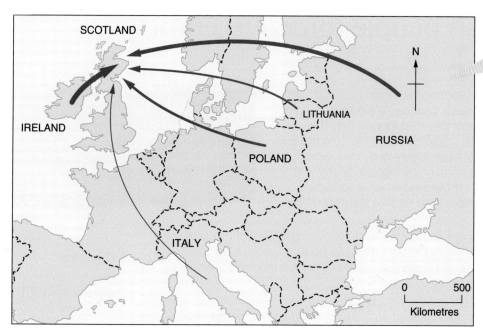

Where immigrants to Scotland came from before 1914.

Where did most European immigrants come from? Describe a possible reason why you think there were more male immigrants than female.

returned to Ireland with the profit from their work. Some of the workers stayed on to be agricultural labourers.

Many Irish people came for the opportunities offered by better jobs and better prospects. Some of these people only intended to stay in Scotland for a short time, until they could afford tickets to take them to destinations like the USA. Gradually, as more Irish people settled in Scotland, it became a magnet for those who wanted a better life. In Scotland it was possible to have a life that still enabled them to stay in touch with their family, their culture and their religion.

Describe why it would have been cheap for Irish people to travel to Scotland.

Where did Irish people settle?

Irish people mostly settled in the west of Scotland and its surrounding area. Areas like Wigtownshire and Dundee also had many Irish people. Irish people settled wherever there were jobs. This meant that areas like Ayrshire (coal) and Dundee (textiles) attracted Irish people because it was possible to get jobs.

So many Irish people settled in Edinburgh that the area around the Cowgate in the city was known as 'Little Ireland'.

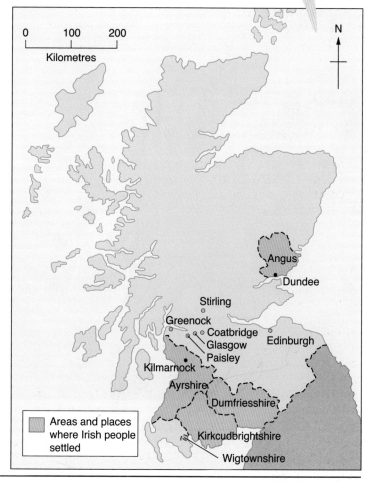

The main areas of where Irish people settled in Scotland.

3

Why were Irish people forced to come to Scotland?

Poverty was the main reason Irish people were forced to come to Scotland – this is called a **push factor**. Most Irish people did not own their own land. From the little money that they earned, they had to pay rent to landlords who often did not live on their lands. If anyone was unable to pay rent, they would be removed from the land and so might emigrate. Many Irish **smallholders** were pushed off the land when landowners wanted to make their own lands bigger so that they could use modern machinery.

> **GLOSSARY**
> **Push factor** a reason that forces people to move abroad
> **Smallholders** farmers renting a small area of land from a landlord

Another reason that Irish people were forced to move was because of the growing population in Ireland. In the 50 years before 1841, the population doubled to eight million. There was not enough agriculture and industry in Ireland to support the population so many had to leave.

> Describe two ways the picture shows how poor farm workers were in Ireland.

The third reason why Irish people left was because of lack of opportunities in Ireland. Irish industry was not growing strongly and so did not provide work. In the nineteenth century, the Irish textile industry suffered in comparison to Britain because British factories made cloth more cheaply. This meant that Irish people working in these industries left to earn more money in Britain.

The interior of an Irish house during the 1830s.

Why did famine cause Irish emigration?

What is potato blight?

Potato blight is a disease that attacks potatoes growing underground and turns them black and uneatable. The potatoes seem to be growing normally but are found to be ruined when it comes to harvest time.

In the mid- and late-1840s, the potato crop in Ireland was destroyed by blight. The worst years were 1845, 1846 and 1848. This caused famine because Ireland's growing population had become dependent on the potato. When the potato crop failed, the Irish people starved. The failure of the potato crop also meant that many people could not pay their rent. When this happened they were evicted from their homes. Landlords used police and soldiers to help them do this. Between 1847 and 1852 there were over 90,000 evictions.

The government system set up to help poor people could not cope with the numbers of people who needed help, which forced some Irish to leave.

A battering ram being used to force an Irish family to leave their home.

Emigrants departing from Queenstown.   Co. Cork.

People departing from Ireland in 1906 by paddle steamer.

What evidence is there in the picture that large numbers of Irish people emigrated?

Why did Irish people come to Scotland to stay?

Permanent large-scale immigration to Scotland happened for two reasons. The first was the Irish famine of 1845–51. The effects on Ireland were devastating; 1–1.5 million Irish people died. A million more emigrated. Most emigrants went to the USA if they could afford it. However, the poorest travelled to places like Scotland and England. They settled in places that were nearest to where the ships reached because they did not have the money for onward travel. In Scotland, this meant that most Irish people settled in the west.

The second reason why Irish people came was because there were jobs available in Scotland – this is called a **pull factor**. This was because Scotland changed economically due to an important event called the **Industrial Revolution**. The Industrial Revolution changed how goods were made. Instead of goods being made at home, factories could produce goods cheaply and quickly. More and more factories needed more and more workers.

One of the first industries to change was the textile industry. This industry made cloth. The factories were powered by water to begin with. The development of the steam engine, powered by coal, meant that factories could be built anywhere, not just near rivers. In Scotland this meant that most factories

> ### GLOSSARY
> **Pull factor** an opportunity that encourages people to move abroad
>
> **Industrial Revolution** a huge change in the economy where new methods are used to make things

were built near to coalfields. These were mostly in the Central Belt of Scotland. Ireland had a profitable textile industry in the eighteenth century but by the nineteenth century it was struggling. Many Irish people came to Scotland where they could get paid more for their skills.

Scottish employers were also happy to attract Irish workers because they worked hard. A farmer's wife was quoted in 'Report on the Irish Poor in Great Britain' as saying:

… her husband has preferred the Irishmen, as harvest labourers, to the Scots or Highlandmen. They work more willingly and labour harder. No Scots reaper he ever had could be compared to an Irish one with his sickle, in the use of which the Irish reapers far surpass the Scots, and also far exceed them in the quantity of corn cut down.

Activity 1

Mindmapping

Put the heading 'Who were the main immigrant groups to Scotland?' in your workbook or work file. Create a mindmap of the main immigrant groups.

Activity 2

Summarise this chapter

▶ Put the heading 'Reasons for Irish immigration to Scotland' in your workbook or work file.
▶ Draw a table like the one below.
▶ Find at least two pieces of information to describe reasons for Irish immigration to Scotland.

	Reasons for Irish immigration to Scotland
Poverty	
Lack of opportunities in Ireland	
Famine	
Cheap transport	
Opportunities in Scotland	

Activity 3

'Walk around, talk around'

Work in pairs or in small groups. Take a large piece of paper and draw a triangle that fills most of the page.

Your teacher will allocate a period of time. Fill the triangle with as many push and pull reasons for Irish people coming to Scotland as possible. Once your time is up, leave your paper and move on to the next group's paper.

Your teacher will allocate another period of time. Add more information to the new group's paper outside the triangle. Keep moving round until all the information is on the paper or the paper is filled.

As a class, discuss and confirm that all main reasons for Irish people coming to Scotland have been included on the papers.

All of the class should take part in discussing and recording information.

Activity 4

Each one, teach one

Find a large space for ease of movement and interaction. On your own, choose a particular fact or event from Activity 3 and write it on a slip of paper. Your teacher may check with you to ensure that there is a spread of different statements across the whole class.

Practise reading your fact or event out loud to check that you understand its meaning.

Draw a clock at the back of your workbook or work file. Put 12, 3, 6 and 9 on the clock. Make 'appointments' with four people in your class for each of these time slots. Your teacher will allocate a period of time for each 'appointment'.

Move around and share your fact or event with your 'appointments', making sure that you explain it fully. Listen to and learn the fact or event that your 'appointment' explains.

Return to your own desk and write down all the facts and events that you have learned in your workbook or work file. You should record at least another three facts or events about why Irish people came to Scotland.

Hold a class discussion on which facts or events were the most interesting and which were easiest or hardest to remember – and why.

Question practice

Source A is about the reasons for Irish emigration to Scotland.

SOURCE A

It was particularly the young adults who left Ireland. For such people the outlook was bad as there were few jobs. There were few cities in Ireland to move to. Therefore the outcome was movement out of Ireland, partly to America but also to Britain because it was cheaper to get to.

1 Explain the reasons for Irish migration. You should use Source A and your own knowledge.

Success criteria

Include at least one factual point of information about the reasons for Irish migration.

Source B is about the reasons Irish people immigrated to Scotland and is based on *The Irish in Scotland* by James Hanley.

SOURCE B

In the years that followed the Great Famine of 1845, the Irish immigrant to Scotland was a poor, starving peasant escaping hunger. In 1845, the potato disease known as blight appeared in Ireland. It was in Ireland that potatoes were the only food for many people. The almost entire failure of the potato crop in the autumn of 1846 following on the partial failure of 1845 increased the numbers of Irish who emigrated to Scotland.

Source C is about the reasons Irish people immigrated to Scotland and is based on *Changing Lives: Scotland and Britain since 1830* by Sydney Wood.

SOURCE C

The Irish population was growing, many people were very poor. At times, especially in the mid-1840s, the failure of the potato crop reduced thousands there to starvation. It was not surprising that so many should cross the Irish Sea to Scotland.

2 Compare the views in Sources B and C about the reasons Irish people immigrated to Scotland. Describe in detail their similarities and/or differences. You can also briefly compare the overall attitude of the sources.

Success criteria

▶ Examine the two sources in order to show two simple points of comparison or one developed point of similarity or difference.
▶ A simple comparison: 'Source B says ... and Source C says ...' will get 1 mark.
▶ A developed comparison: 'Sources B and C agree that the failure of the potato crop in 1845 and 1846 was a key reason for people leaving Ireland. Source B says ... and Source C says ...' will get 2 marks.

National 5

1 Explain the reasons why so many Irish people immigrated to Scotland. (5 marks)

This is an 'explain' question. That means you must give five reasons why something did or did not happen. It is not enough just to write down facts no matter how correct they are. You must make clear exactly how these facts did or did not allow something to happen. In terms of this question your writing must use facts to show why so many Irish people came to Scotland.

There will not be a source in the exam to help you, but to get you started on your answer here are some hints:

- Explain why poverty caused Irish people to come to Scotland.
- Explain why the Irish potato famine caused Irish people to come to Scotland.
- Explain why the slow response of the British government caused Irish people to emigrate to Scotland.
- Explain why the lack of opportunities in Ireland caused people to emigrate.
- Explain why Scotland attracted Irish people to come and live there.
- Explain why transport links led many Irish people to come to Scotland.

Success criteria

- Include five factual pieces of information on why so many Irish people came to Scotland or include at least three developed pieces of information on why so many Irish people came to Scotland.
- Give accurate and detailed pieces of information that are properly explained.

Source A is about why Irish people came to Scotland and is from *The Great Irish Famine and Scottish History* by T.M. Devine.

SOURCE A

The movement of Irish famine refugees to Scotland was less significant than elsewhere because fewer than 100,000 came to Scotland during the crisis years. However, this was an enormous burden for a small country which contained only around 2.8 million inhabitants in 1845. The poorer refugees opted for the British mainland because of quicker access and cheaper fares. The famine migrations seem to have been mainly Catholic from the poorer areas of Ireland. The failure of the potatoes which triggered the catastrophe seemed unending. Rather than a one-off crisis in 1845 and 1846 there was another massive shortage in 1848.

2 How fully does Source A show the reasons why so many Irish came to Scotland? You should use Source A and your own knowledge. (6 marks)

This is a 'how fully' question. In this type of question you need to select the points from the source which are relevant to the question – usually there will be three points in the source. Then, to get full marks you need to bring in points from recall that are also relevant to the question.

Success criteria

- Place the source in context by explaining information in the source and applying that information to your own knowledge.
- A maximum of 2 marks may be given for answers in which no judgement has been made.
- Up to 3 marks can be gained for explaining points of information from the source.
- Up to 4 marks can be gained for explaining points of information from your own knowledge which are relevant to the question asked.
- Pieces of information from your own knowledge can act either as further explanation of points of information from the source or as new points.

Chapter 3 Why did other immigrant groups come to Scotland?

What is this chapter about?

The largest immigrant group to come to Scotland was Irish, but other people who came included Lithuanians, Italians and Jewish people. They migrated for a number of reasons: some came to work and others came to escape persecution. The one thing that they had in common was that they all made Scotland their home.

By the end of this chapter you should be able to:

▶ Explain why Lithuanians, Italians and Jewish people came to Scotland.
▶ Describe where these groups settled.
▶ Explain which other groups came to Scotland and why they came.

Why did Lithuanians come to Scotland and where did they settle?

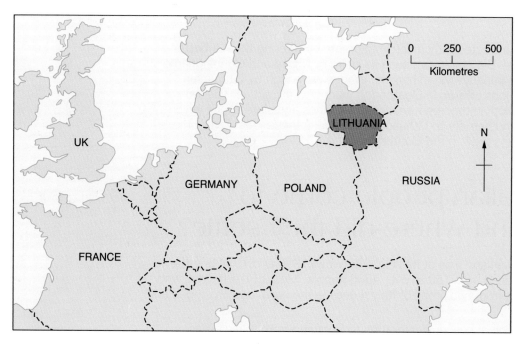

Lithuania was part of the Russian Empire at this time.

In the 1890s, large numbers of Lithuanians came to Scotland. They were attracted by work in the coalmines and the iron and steel works around Coatbridge near Glasgow. By 1914, there were around 5000–6000 Lithuanians living in Scotland.

What does such a photograph tell us about the Lithuanian community in Scotland?

Lithuanian women working in a coal mine.

Most of the Lithuanians came to Scotland for economic reasons. Many came from farming backgrounds where it was extremely hard to make a living because the landholdings were so small and the farming methods basic. Other Lithuanians were forced to leave because of persecution by the Russian government. At that time, Lithuania was part of Russia.

Most of the Lithuanian emigrants hoped to reach the USA. They came to Scotland as a stepping-stone because there was a well-established shipping route that linked Europe to Scotland and then to the rest of the world.

Lithuanians also came to Scotland because employers in Scotland tried to attract Lithuanians to come and work here. This account is by a Lithuanian immigrant on how Lithuanians were persuaded to go to Scotland:

Our parents told us that the iron masters in Coatbridge went to Lithuania recruiting men to dig coal … and paid their fare over to this country only … Well, they had no money to leave, or even to go on to America, or leave here and go back to their own country.

Employers in Scotland attracted Lithuanian immigrants by offering them a better life and a brighter future. Big employers such as Baird or Merry and Cunninghame in Coatbridge offered company-owned houses. Wages were high by Lithuanian standards. The type of jobs offered in Coatbridge were also attractive. The jobs were mostly unskilled work in the iron furnaces, coal mines and slate mines which meant that there were no barriers to Lithuanians taking up these jobs. Over time, a community of Lithuanians grew in the Coatbridge area.

Why did Italian people come to Scotland and where did they settle?

Italian immigration to Scotland was at its height between 1890 and 1914 and the Italian population increased from 750 to over 4500 people. Most of the Italians who came to Scotland came from two areas of Italy: Lucca in the north and Frosinone and Abruzzo in the south.

There was a long tradition of seasonal migration to Scotland from these areas. However, when the population of Italy increased in the late nineteenth century, it became harder to make a living. Some people left Italy and some of these people found their way to Scotland.

An Italian who immigrated to Scotland recalled:

*My father had eight of a family. He was a **peasant** and of course somebody had to go out, you know, of the family. So he says 'You canna make a living here … so some of you has got to go somewhere else to make a start in life.' I was glad to come here [Cambuslang], I mean to make some kinda progress in life for my ambition was to live the proper way, no' the rough way …*

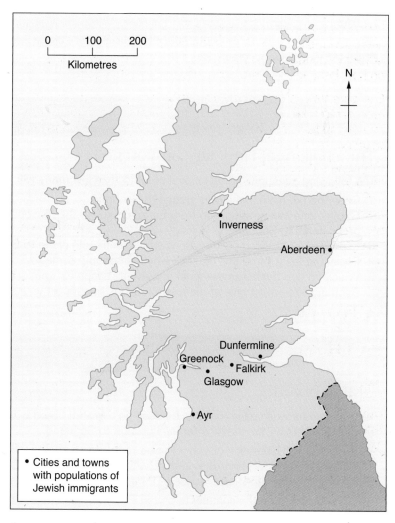

GLOSSARY

Peasant someone who makes their living from farming a small piece of land

Migrants people who travel from one place to another, often in search of work

Yiddish a language spoken by Jews

Italians were also attracted to Scotland by recruiting agents working for *padroni* (employers or patrons) based in London. Often, these *padroni* worked in the ice-cream trade, which is why Italians came to be so connected with this business.

Italians settled all over Scotland, and Italian ice-cream shops and fish and chip shops became common in most towns and villages across Scotland. There were also fairly large Italian communities in all the main cities like Glasgow and Edinburgh.

Why did Jewish people come to Scotland and where did they settle?

Jews had migrated to Scotland for many years. At first, Jewish immigrants tended to be educated and wealthy. From the mid-1870s and 1880s, many Jews came to Scotland to escape persecution and poverty in eastern Europe. Most of the Jewish **migrants** then sailed on to start a new life in the USA, but some settled in Scotland.

In Scotland, Jews settled in the big cities, especially Glasgow. In 1914, there were more than 7000 Jews in Glasgow (0.9 per cent of the total population). There were two different kinds of Jewish immigrants: well-educated people who tended to live north of the River Clyde, and **Yiddish**-speaking Jews from Poland and Russia. This latter group settled in the cheaper Gorbals district of the city. In 1939, the Jewish population of Glasgow increased as Jewish men, women and children escaped Nazi Germany and Austria.

Ayr, Aberdeen, Dunfermline, Falkirk, Greenock and Inverness also become home to Jewish families. It is possible to see evidence of Jewish communities through the synagogues built for Jewish religious gatherings and the facilities that provided religious education for Jewish children. The facilities aimed to protect Jewish culture.

Cities and towns in Scotland with populations of Jewish immigrants.

Why did other groups come to Scotland?

By far the biggest immigrant group to Scotland was people from England. The reasons for English people settling and the patterns of settlement have not attracted the same attention as other immigrant groups. However, it seems likely that English people moved to Scotland for the same reasons that other groups did: opportunities and jobs. In the nineteenth century, Scotland had a thriving engineering and shipping industry. Some of Scotland's companies were international and so would have attracted people from England for the career opportunities they offered.

Activity 1

Summarise this chapter

The following summary reminds you of what this chapter has been about. Words that are important have been made into ANAGRAMS. Your task is to sort out the anagrams and then write the correct version of this summary into your workbook or work file.

Other than **ISHIR** people, the main immigration groups were **ATIALNI, HJIESW** and **UTANIAILNH** people. Most came to Scotland for a mixture of reasons. Some were escaping **YOVPERT**, others were escaping **CUTPERSENIO**. Immigrants chose Scotland because of easy **PORTNASTR** and job opportunities.

Activity 2

The challenge! How far can you go?

The following questions go up in level of difficulty. How many will you try to do?

1 Describe the main immigrant groups to Scotland.
2 Choose one immigrant group from Europe. Explain the reasons why this immigrant group came to Scotland.
3 Explain at least three push reasons why Irish people came to Scotland.
4 Explain at least three pull reasons why Irish people came to Scotland.
5 Which do you think was the most important reason for immigrants coming to Scotland? You must give at least two reasons to support your answer.

Activity 3

Graffiti board

You will need a wall space that can be used as a graffiti board where you can write and record thoughts on the reasons for immigration to Scotland.

Your teacher will give each of you a Post-it note. Write one question or piece of information you know about the reasons why Italians, Jews and Lithuanians came to Scotland. Add one question or piece of information you would like to find out about.

Hold a discussion on the comments on the Post-it notes and put the notes onto the graffiti board. When everyone has finished, take another Post-it note and record what you have learned about reasons for immigration to Scotland.

Question practice

National 4

Source A is one person's view about the reasons why Italian people came to Scotland.

SOURCE A

There was poverty in Italy. It was a terrible struggle. If someone took ill or if someone needed an operation, you had to sell a cow or sell one of your mules. That was a great hardship because they would need it. Everyone was glad to escape the hard life they had over in Italy.

Explain the reasons for Italian immigration to Scotland. You should use Source A and your own knowledge.

Success criteria

Include at least one factual point of information about why Italians came over to Scotland.

National 5

Source A is from a Jewish immigrant to Scotland remembering her childhood.

SOURCE A

I come frae Dubna guberniya [region] in Russia and I was born, I think, in 1891. I remember that I was always running around, going to the market. Everybody was poor. The **pogroms** *were getting so bad that I was told they used to go into a house and they'd pull a baby's tongue out! I was told that and I felt terrible and I thought I'd like to see what these people looked like, but they were just ordinary soldiers. Anyway people were nervous in case things got worse and that's the reason they left because things weren't so good.*

1 Evaluate the usefulness of Source A as evidence of the reasons for Jewish immigration to Scotland. You may want to comment on who wrote it, when they wrote it, why they wrote it, what they say or what has been missed out.
(6 marks)

GLOSSARY

Pogrom an organised attack on Jews

Success criteria

- To get 1 mark, you need to explain the importance of each of the points you make about the source.
- Up to 4 marks may be given for evaluative comments about origin and purpose. Comments about the origin may include an explanation about the type of source, the author or the timing of the source. Comments about purpose may include an explanation about why the source was written.
- Up to 2 marks may be given for your evaluation of the content of the source which you consider is useful in terms of the proposed question. For full marks to be given, each point needs to be discretely mentioned and its usefulness explained.
- If you list information, that will be considered to be one point and will get only 1 mark.
- Up to 2 marks may be given for evaluative comments relating to points of information not mentioned in the source.

Source B is about Jewish immigration to Scotland and is from *Second City Jewry* by Kenneth E. Collins.

SOURCE B

The flow of Jews along emigration routes through Scotland was to increase after 1880. There were some Jews from eastern Europe who were settling in Glasgow rather than continuing their journey, as well as other Jews who were arriving in Glasgow from other centres in Britain attracted by the increasing economic opportunities. The emigration of Jews from Russian Poland and Lithuania to Scotland owed as much to unsettled economic conditions as it did to increasing levels of **anti-Semitism**, *which might include the brutal violence of the pogrom.*

Source C is also about Jewish immigration to Scotland and is from *Jews in Glasgow, 1879–1939* by Ben Braber.

> **GLOSSARY**
> **Anti-Semitism** hatred of Jews

SOURCE C

The Clyde was the ultimate reason why migrants came to Glasgow. The river was an outlet for people leaving Europe and an economic lifeline for those who stayed in the Scottish city. The Jewish migrants formed part of a large population movement from central and eastern Europe to western European countries. Underlying the general mass migration was the pressure of a fast growing population with apparently better economic prospects in the west. The fear of pogroms also drove people to emigrate.

2 Compare the views of Sources B and C on the reasons for immigration to Scotland. **(4 marks)**

Success criteria

- You should interpret evidence from the sources and make direct comparisons between the information in the sources.
- You can get up to 4 marks for making four simple comparisons between the information in the two sources.
- You can get up to 4 marks for making two developed comparisons between the sources.
- A simple comparison: 'Source B says … and Source C says …' will get 1 mark. A developed comparison: 'Sources B and C agree about economic reasons for immigration to Scotland. Source B says … and Source C says …' will get 2 marks.

3 To what extent was poverty the main reason why immigrants came to Scotland between 1830 and 1939? **(8 marks)**

To be successful in this type of question, your answer should include:

- A judgement about the main reasons for immigration to Scotland.
- A paragraph discussing evidence for push and pull reasons why Irish people came to Scotland.
- A paragraph discussing some evidence and differing reasons why Jewish, Lithuanian and Italian people came to Scotland.
- A reasoned conclusion based on the evidence presented that addresses the question.

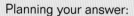

Planning your answer:

- In small groups or pairs, mindmap the information on push and pull reasons why Irish people came to Scotland and the differing reasons why Jewish, Lithuanian and Italian people came to Scotland.
- Group the information into 'poverty reasons' and 'other reasons' paragraphs.
- Find connections between the different pieces of information and group them together. This will give you a structure for the order in which you talk about the significance of poverty as a reason for immigrant groups coming to Scotland.
- Plan an overall response to the question.
- Show your plan to your teacher before starting your first draft.
- Carefully check your first draft.
- Rewrite the final draft of your answer.

Success criteria

Knowledge:

- Make a judgement about why immigrants came to Scotland between 1830 and 1939.
- Your answer must provide a balanced account of the different reasons immigrants came to Scotland between 1830 and 1939 and come to a reasoned conclusion based on the evidence presented.
- Up to 5 marks are given for relevant points used to address the question.
- 1 mark will be given for each accurate point that is properly explained.
- You can get 1 further mark for each point by developing its detail or explanation.
- A maximum of 3 marks is allocated for relevant knowledge used to address the question where only one factor or only one side of the argument is presented.

Structure:

Up to 3 marks can be given for presenting the answer in a structured way, leading to a reasoned conclusion that answers the question.

- 1 mark for the answer being presented in a structured way. The information should be organised and mention different factors.
- 1 mark for a valid judgement or overall conclusion.
- 1 mark for a reason being provided in support of the conclusion.

Chapter 4 Did the British Empire benefit Scotland?

What is this chapter about?

Many Scots who emigrated did not stay in the countries they moved to and returned home to Scotland. They brought money and new experiences with them. Being part of the British Empire had both good and bad effects on Scotland.

By the end of this chapter you should be able to:

▶ Describe the positive effects of the British Empire on Scotland.
▶ Explain the negative effects of the British Empire on Scotland.

What were the positive effects of the British Empire on Scotland?

There were a number of ways in which the **British Empire** had a positive effect on Scotland. It brought new ideas and religions, increasing Scotland's variety as a country. It can also be argued that the Empire enhanced sport and recreation; the rivalry between teams like Rangers and Celtic helped to create a more vibrant football league. The people who came to Scotland also brought new influences on the style of buildings and architecture.

> ### GLOSSARY
>
> **British Empire** the network of land and countries controlled by Britain from 1830 to 1939

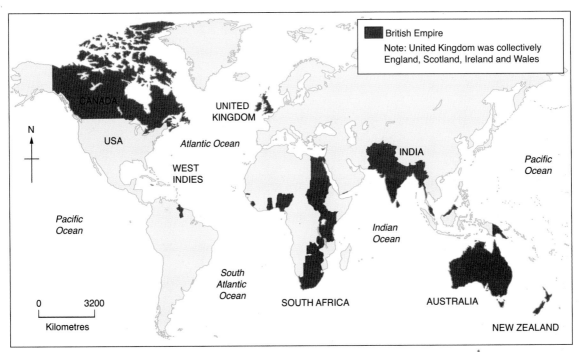

The British Empire around 1830.

Importantly, the Empire increased the industry and wealth of cities like Glasgow, which became known as the 'second city of the Empire'. As a result of the money from Empire trade, Glasgow was able to build famous public buildings such as the Kelvingrove Museum. The museum was built from the profits of the 1888 international exhibition in Kelvingrove Park, which had been held to celebrate the city's achievements in the sciences, industry and art during the Industrial Revolution. Two-thirds of the industry exhibitors at the exhibition were from Scotland. One of them, Doulton & Co., built the world's largest terracotta fountain, which can still be seen in Glasgow today.

Immigrants from the Empire also provided a workforce that was willing to work for low wages and so helped Scotland's industry to increase. The contribution of Irish people to Scotland's economic growth was especially important in this respect. Also, the Empire provided raw materials for factories, such as cotton and jute. Dundee textile firms became internationally known as a result. For many, the most obvious effects of Empire on Scotland were the jobs and opportunities for Scots abroad. Scots were very quick to take up jobs overseas either in private firms or for the government. Scottish soldiers and civil servants became very well known for running the **colonies** of the British Empire.

> ## GLOSSARY
> **Colonies** land or territories controlled by another country, usually a western European one

Kelvingrove Museum.

What evidence can you see in the fountain of Glasgow's links with the Empire?

The Doulton Fountain in Glasgow.

The Empire provided a market for Scottish goods and emigrants.

William Teacher (1811–76) worked in a small grocer's shop in Anderston and married the owner's daughter in 1834. He expanded the business with a chain of wine and spirit shops and in the 1850s began to open public houses known as 'dram shops' where customers could drink whisky. Teacher's dram shops maintained strict rules forbidding customers from smoking and buying rounds, and anyone 'under the influence' could expect to be ejected from the premises by one of the Highlanders that Teacher liked to employ as barmen. The main attraction of the dram shops was their reputation for providing customers with high-quality whisky.

Teacher entered the whisky wholesale and blending business and Teacher's Highland Cream became a leading Scotch whisky brand. In 1898–9, Teacher's built the Ardmore distillery in Aberdeenshire.

The Empire also helped Scotland to develop as an export economy, especially with industries like ships and railway engines. A huge number of Glasgow's businesses depended on exports. As well as shipbuilding and railways, Glasgow firms sent products as different as bridges and bandstands, stoves and steam hammers around the world.

Look at all the references to Scotland in the poster. What does this tell you about how people thought about Scotland?

An advertisement for Teacher's Scotch whisky, 1900s.

A locomotive made by the North British Locomotive Company of Glasgow, being hoisted on board a ship for transport to Egypt, part of a consignment of 20 being shipped at a rate of eight a month.

What were the negative effects of the Empire on Scotland?

There were a number of ways in which the British Empire had a negative effect on Scotland.

Large numbers of poorer immigrants arrived in Scotland from the 1840s onwards. Their arrival tended to make health and housing problems worse because there was little government action to address these problems until later.

Immigrants brought their own religion and ideas with them, which sometimes caused problems in Scotland. For example, Irish immigration to Scotland brought the **sectarian rivalries** between Catholic and Protestant Christianity. The religious divisions between Catholics and Protestants helped to create an unequal education system for the two communities. It was not until 1918 that Catholics got equal access to state education.

> **GLOSSARY**
>
> **Sectarian rivalries** divisions between two communities, usually over religion and ideas

Large numbers of Scots moved abroad to countries within the Empire. Most of those Scots who left were fairly well-educated young people from the Central Belt area. Their talents were therefore lost to Scotland in helping build up its industry and economy. Areas like the Highlands were devastated by the continued emigration of its people between 1839 and 1939. The **depopulation** of the Highlands had a severe impact on the economy of the area, leading to continued problems even to the present day.

> **GLOSSARY**
>
> **Depopulation** migration or emigration leading to a decrease in population

It can be argued that the Empire inflated the Scottish economy and made it over-dependent on exports. This meant that in times of world economic downturn, such as after the First World War, Scotland suffered more than it might otherwise have done.

The Empire created competition for Scottish goods and products. Over time, other countries in the Empire were able to produce goods more cheaply and undercut Scottish factories and jobs. Industries where this happened were sheep farming in Australia and New Zealand and the linen and jute industry in India. By the twentieth century, linen production in Dundee suffered from competition from factories in India that were making their own jute products. The jute industry in Dundee survived a little longer but mainly because of the two world wars which created a demand for sandbags.

Activity 1

'Walk around, talk around'

Work in pairs or in small groups. Take a large piece of paper and draw a triangle that fills most of the page.

Your teacher will allocate a period of time. Fill the triangle with as much information as you can with as many positive and negative effects of the British Empire on Scotland as possible. Once your time is up, leave your paper and move on to the next group's paper.

Your teacher will allocate another period of time. Add more information to the new group's paper outside the triangle. Keep moving round until all the information is on the paper or the paper is filled.

As a class, discuss and confirm that all the effects of the British Empire on Scotland have been included on the papers.

All of the class should take part in discussing and recording information.

Activity 2

Two stars and a wish

This is a group activity and should be done in small groups. This task asks you to 'consider all factors' and reach a conclusion on the extent to which the British Empire had a positive effect on Scotland.

Take your large sheet of paper from Activity 1 and place all the different effects of the Empire on Scotland under different factors, for example, religion, industry, jobs and so on. You might add your own factors. Make a copy and fill out the template below for each factor in your workbook or work file.

Template

Question to be discussed: …

Factor 1:   Positive impact on Scotland: …

              Negative impact on Scotland: …

              Key evidence: …

Question to be discussed: …

Factor 2:   Positive impact on Scotland: …

              Negative impact on Scotland: …

              Key evidence: …

Question to be discussed:

Factor 3:   Positive impact on Scotland: …

              Negative impact on Scotland: …

              Key evidence: …

Rotate in groups to view the factors that the other groups have noted. Give each template a peer review: 'two stars and a wish'. This means that you should award a star for each piece of quality information to a maximum of two and one wish on what could be added to improve the template. Return to your own template and update your original factors based on what other groups have written in their templates.

Question practice

National 4

Source A is about the impact of the British Empire on Scotland.

SOURCE A

Scotland got access to the British Empire after 1707. The Empire had varied effects on Scotland. On the one hand, it gave ambitious Scots the chance of owning their own lands. It also provided Scots at home with jobs from industries that traded with the Empire. On the other hand, the Empire competed with Scottish companies in industries like linen and jute.

Describe the impact of the British Empire on Scotland. You should use Source A and your own knowledge.

Success criteria

Include at least two factual points of information, or one developed piece of information about the impact of the Empire on Scotland.

National 5

1 Describe the impact of the British Empire on Scotland between 1830 and 1939. **(5 marks)**

There will not be a source in the exam to help you, but to get you started on your answer here are some hints:

▶ Describe the positive effects of the British Empire on Scottish jobs.
▶ Describe the negative effects of the British Empire on Scottish jobs.
▶ Describe the positive effects of emigration for Scots.
▶ Describe the negative effects of emigration on the Highlands and Scotland.
▶ Describe the positive effects of new religion and ideas on Scotland.
▶ Describe the negative effects of new religion and ideas on Scotland.
▶ Describe the positive effects of the British Empire on Scottish industry.
▶ Describe the negative effects of the British Empire on Scottish industry.

Success criteria

▶ Provide five factual points of information on the impact of the Empire on Scotland between 1830 and 1939 or include at least three developed pieces of information.
▶ Give accurate and detailed pieces of information that are properly explained.

Source A is about the impact of the British Empire on Scotland.

SOURCE A

Glasgow was at the peak of its self-confidence in the nineteenth century. Its population had passed that of Edinburgh by the 1821 census and soon after it was referring to itself as the 'second city of the Empire'. By the 1880s, fine classical buildings as statements of power and wealth were appearing along fine new streets. Population increased five-fold. By the end of the century it was also claiming to be the best governed city in Europe. Its cultural life was vibrant and creative.

2 How fully does Source A show the impact of the British Empire on Scotland? You should use Source A and your own knowledge. **(6 marks)**

Success criteria

▶ Place the source in context by explaining information in the source and applying that information to your own knowledge.
▶ A maximum of 2 marks may be given for answers in which no judgement has been made.
▶ Up to 3 marks can be gained for explaining pieces of information from the source.
▶ Up to 4 marks can be gained for explaining pieces of information from your own knowledge which are relevant to the question asked.
▶ Pieces of information from your own knowledge can act either as further explanation of pieces of information from the source or as new points.

Chapter 5 What was life like for Irish immigrants coming to Scotland?

What is this chapter about?

By the 1880s, large numbers of Irish people were living in Scotland. The census of 1881 shows that 218,745 Irish people were born in Scotland. This figure fell to 124,296 by 1931. Irish immigrants worked in a number of different jobs in Scotland. Their contribution to the economic development of Scotland was important. They often lived in the poorer areas of Scotland's cities. Most of the Irish people who came to Scotland were Catholic, but there were also a large number of Protestants. Their relationship with the Scottish people was not good to start with, but this changed over time. Some Irish immigrants became important political leaders in Scotland.

By the end of this chapter you should be able to:

- Describe what it was like for Irish people living in Scotland.
- Describe the different sorts of jobs done by Irish immigrants.
- Explain why Scots were not always friendly towards the new immigrants.

What sorts of jobs did Irish people do?

By the 1880s, Irish immigrants had found permanent jobs in a number of Scottish industries. Irish workers were employed in coal mines, iron works and the factories of Scotland. Irish workers also helped build the canals and railways that would provide transport for the people and trade for Scotland.

Of course, permanent jobs meant that Irish immigrants settled in Scotland. Irish workers were concentrated in Glasgow and the west of Scotland. Towns like Airdrie, Coatbridge and Larkhall saw large numbers of Irish people settle in them. However, large numbers of Irish people also worked in the jute mills of Dundee, the breweries of Edinburgh and the mining areas of Lothian, in the east of Scotland.

To begin with, many of the Irish people were employed in the cotton industry, settling in the cloth-producing towns of Ayrshire and Lanarkshire, but it is in the heavy industries of coal mining and iron-making, and as **navvies**, building the railways, that Irish people are most remembered.

The first public railway in Scotland was a 10-mile (16-km) line that opened in 1826. It ran between Monkland and Kirkintilloch. By the 1880s, Scotland's towns, cities and many villages were connected by a vast system of railway lines. Many of the men who built these railways came from Ireland.

> **GLOSSARY**
>
> **Navvies** short for navigators; people who work as labourers on road or rail building, for example

What were living conditions like for Irish immigrants?

The Industrial Revolution meant that many people moved to Scotland's cities to find work. Housing conditions were poor as a result. Homes consisted of overcrowded tenements along narrow streets. The streets were open sewers. The water supply was mixed with human waste. Overcrowding, a lack of clean water and poor sanitation led to disease. Irish immigrants lived in these slum conditions because they were poor and the housing was cheap.

The immigrant Irish people lived in the poorer parts of Scotland's cities. In Edinburgh, Irish immigrants concentrated in the Old Town in the Cowgate and Grassmarket areas. Eventually there were so many Irish people living in this area that the local Edinburgh people called it 'Little Ireland' or 'Little Dublin'. In Glasgow, Irish immigrants concentrated in the slums of the Saltmarket, Cowcaddens and Maryhill. In Dundee it was the Lochee area.

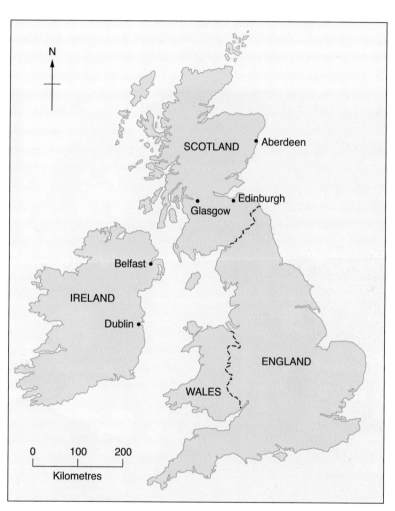

The map shows how close Ireland and Scotland are.

The housing conditions in Glasgow and the people who lived in them were described by a journalist in 1890:

Men and women living in a chronic state, until they could hardly be recognised as human, picking up food that even animals will turn away from. There were dwellings sleeping 50, 60, 80 people all together, of all ages and both sexes, in a room that could not hold ten with decency, swearing, fighting, trampling on one another, filling the room with foul air. This is not a picture of occasional misery, in some places it represents everyday life.

Unfortunately, many Scots blamed the Irish people for causing problems in the areas where they lived. It is true that in such conditions some Irish immigrants drank alcohol in order to forget and escape their everyday life – so the Irish people were labelled as heavy drinkers. It was also true that the slums led to deadly diseases, such as typhus, spreading among the population but it was not true that Irish people caused the diseases – although many Scots believed that they did!

Historian Christopher Smout explains why people held these beliefs:

For the unskilled on low or irregular wages it was difficult to keep up a respectable lifestyle however hard you saved. It was so much more tempting to spend everything on a horse or a night's drinking. As a result, labourers, and the Irish in particular, came to have a reputation for fighting, drunkenness and general 'bad' behaviour.

> Identify as many points as you can from the photograph that show the poverty of the family that lived there.

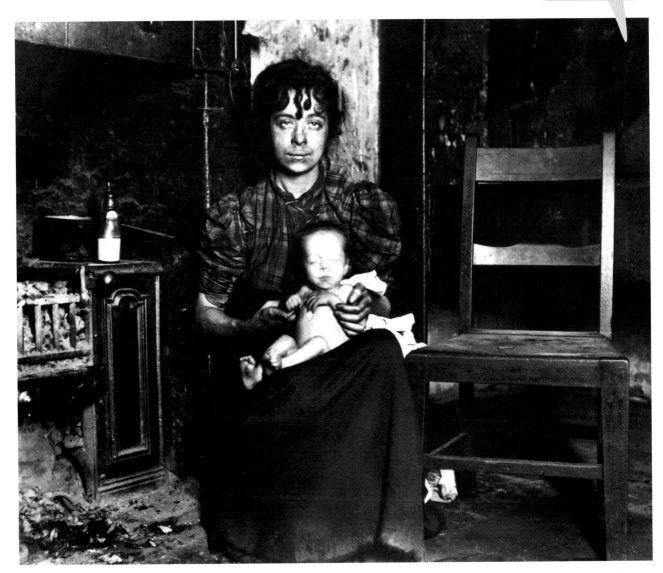

Inside a slum tenement in Glasgow around 1910.

How can you tell the cartoon is against the Irish?

Were Irish immigrants really all that different from Scots?

Many immigrants like to live near people who speak the same language, have the same customs and religion, and are employed in similar jobs. The Irish immigrants were no different. The Irish people had their own culture, social customs and habits. Some even spoke a different language. In other words, the Irish immigrants had their own identity. They were different from Scots. Many Scots reacted badly to what they saw as an 'alien' invasion.

Both the Irish Catholics and Protestants shared certain customs and habits that made them different from the Scottish population. Seventy-five per cent of the Irish immigrants were Catholic. Religion mattered because in 1880 most Scots belonged to the Protestant Church. Many Scots saw large numbers of Catholic Irish as a threat. For example, the number of Catholic priests in the city of Glasgow grew from 134 in 1878 to 234 in 1902. This meant that many more Catholics were arriving and needing the help of **parish** priests.

Young Catholics were encouraged to socialise in the Church. Organisations to help Catholics in Scotland developed. The St Vincent de Paul Society helped the poor. The League of the Cross tackled the problem of alcohol. Even football clubs were developed. Celtic Football Club was founded by Brother Walfrid in 1887. Edinburgh Hibernian and Dundee Harp are two other football clubs started by Irish Catholic communities in Scotland.

'The Order of the Day; Or, Unions and **Fenians**.' Irish people were seen as dangerous by many people in Britain.

GLOSSARY

Parish a small district, normally with its own church and a priest or church minister

Fenians organisations that wanted Ireland to be independent from Britain

A parade of the Irish National Foresters through Penicuik, near Edinburgh, in the late nineteenth century. There were branches of the organisation across Scotland. This is a good example of an organisation created by Irish Catholics in Scotland. It died out after the Irish Free State was created in 1922.

Separate Catholic schools also played their part in reinforcing Catholic identity and marking out Catholic children as different from the mainly Protestant Scots. To begin with, these schools were funded by donations from the local Catholic community. In 1918, Catholic schools began to get money from the government. The 1918 Education (Scotland) Act allowed Catholic schools to join the government-funded education system. Protestant groups complained that this was special treatment and was unfair. Some complained of the use of local property taxes (called rates) to pay for Catholic schools. Those schools meant that the children of Irish Catholic families did not mix with local children so the differences between Protestant Scots and Catholic Irish continued.

Protestant Irish people shared their religion with the majority of Scots but they also created their own separate identity with something that still exists in Scotland today – the Loyal Orange Order. The growth of the Orange Movement in Scotland is another effect of Irish Protestant immigration. Irish Protestants brought the Orange Lodge with them to Scotland and by 1880 lodges were well established in the west of Scotland around the Glasgow area. The lodges provided an important social function and reinforced Protestant Irish identity with annual marches on 12 July. These marches celebrate Protestant influence and remain controversial even today.

Were Irish immigrants treated badly by Scots?

To begin with, relations between the immigrant Irish and local Scots were not good. The Irish people gained a reputation as **strike** breakers – people who took the jobs of striking workers. To fight back against the strike, the employer would hire new workers who agreed to work for less money than the strikers got. By doing this, the employer could keep his business operating and the strike would collapse. Workers who struggled for better wages and working conditions hated strike breakers. In fact, the role of Irish workers as strike breakers was common only in the coal and iron industries.

Irish navvies gained a particularly bad reputation for drunken behaviour. Local newspapers described the navvies as, 'swarms of wild Irishmen'. There is evidence of fighting and even riots between Irish navvies and the local population in towns like Kelso and Dunfermline. The navvies even fought amongst themselves.

Religion was another reason that the Irish were considered a problem by the Scots. The arrival of large numbers of Irish Catholics led to the belief that they were a threat to the Protestant Scottish way of life. People who believed this were prejudiced against the Catholic Irish. Organisations developed that were opposed to Catholics, these included the Scottish Reformation Society, founded in 1850, and the Protestant Action Society, which was active in Edinburgh in the 1930s. Irish Catholics were accused of not having any loyalty to Scotland. They were said to be loyal to the Pope instead.

> ## GLOSSARY
>
> **Strike** when workers stop working, usually to try to force an employer to pay higher wages
>
> **Assimilated** people of different backgrounds becoming part of a larger national family
>
> **Trade union** a workers' organisation that aims to protect members' pay and conditions

Did relations between Irish and Scots improve by the 1930s?

The short answer is both yes and no.

In 1923, the Church of Scotland published a pamphlet called 'The Menace of the Irish Race to our Scottish Nationality'. This shows that anti-Catholic feeling continued to exist in Scotland at this time.

Some Scottish politicians agreed. In 1932, the Conservative Member of Parliament for Perth told Parliament that:

Culturally the Irish population has not been **assimilated** *into the Scottish population. There is in the west of Scotland a completely separate race of alien origin whose presence there is bitterly resented by tens of thousands of the Scottish working class.*

However, there is evidence that not all relations were bad. Concern about the amount of alcohol consumed in Scotland led to the development of the Temperance Movement. Members of the Temperance Movement took a pledge not to drink alcohol. There is a great deal of evidence that the Catholic and Protestant communities joined together in order to tackle the troubles caused by excessive drinking.

There were also important links through the **trade union** movement. Working-class Irish and Scottish people faced the same problems over pay and working conditions. One industry that saw a growth in Irish influence was mining. Miners' trade unions

The Menance of the Irish Race to our Scottish Nationality

Be Scotland still to Scotland true,
Amang oursels united!
For never but by Scottish hands
Maun Scottish wrangs be righted.
—*After Robert Burns*.

The Report to the General Assembly of the Church of Scotland on the Irish Problem in Scotland. Notes taken from Official Sources being added.

EDINBURGH
1923

The cover of the Church of Scotland's pamphlet called 'The Menace of the Irish Race to our Scottish Nationality'.

saw a growth in Irish workers joining. By 1900, Irish people made up about 75 per cent of the membership of the Lanarkshire miners' union.

As well as links through the Temperance Movement and trade unionism, many Irish immigrants seem to have got on very well with the local Scots. There is evidence of **intermarriage** between Irish Catholics and local Scottish people. However, mixed marriages between Protestant Scots and Catholic Irish also concerned the Catholic Church. One of the reasons that the Catholic Church encouraged Catholic men and women to socialise together in halls attached to Catholic chapels was to try to prevent them from meeting Protestants.

Eventually, the shared experience of working together and of involvement in the First World War meant that the idea of seeing the Irish community as something separate did reduce. However, it has not gone entirely away. As recently as 8 January 2013, the Catholic Church's spokesman, Peter Kearney, raised the problem of anti-Catholic discrimination in Scotland.

> **GLOSSARY**
> **Intermarriage** marriage between races or religions

How important was Irish Immigration to the economic growth of Scotland?

Irish immigrants, both Catholic and Protestant, were very important in the economic development of Scotland. Evidence from employers generally agrees with this.

Many historians also agree that the Irish were very important in the economic development of Scotland. Historian Tom Devine states:

The huge construction schemes of the nineteenth-century cities and the building of roads, railways, canals, docks and harbours depended on this vast supply of Irish workers.

Irish people mostly worked in unskilled manual industries. There is also evidence of many Protestant Irish workers being deliberately recruited by Scottish engineering and shipbuilding firms. These were skilled jobs. Towns like Coatbridge and Larkhall were centres for the iron industry. The iron-founding firm of William Baird & Co. advertised for workers in Belfast newspapers. This shows that the Irish were not only important as muscle to build industrial Scotland, but that skilled workers were also needed and recruited from Ireland.

What effect did Irish immigration have on Scottish politics?

At the start of the First World War, many Irish men living in Scotland joined the armed forces to fight for Britain against Germany. This helped to bond Irish and Scots together. However, events in Dublin in 1916 were to change things.

Sinn Féin was a political party in Ireland that wanted full independence from Britain. In 1916, at Easter, Sinn Féin attempted to start a rebellion against Britain by launching an armed uprising in Dublin. This was later called the Easter Rising. The leaders of the rebellion were caught, tried and then executed by order of the British government. Although most Irish people did not support the uprising, these events led to a massive growth of support for Sinn Féin in Ireland and Scotland. By 1920, there were 80 Sinn Féin clubs in Scotland. These clubs raised money to support the cause of Irish independence.

The south of Ireland became independent from Britain in 1922. This was important in Scotland. Irish Catholics in Scotland had supported the Liberal Party because the Liberals had promoted the idea of the Irish ruling themselves. When a large part of Ireland became independent, this link was broken and many Irish Catholics switched their support to the Labour Party. As many Irish people were trade union members and worked in badly paid industries, this change of politics was perhaps expected as Labour supported workers and their rights to better pay and conditions.

The Protestant Irish community, on the other side of the Irish political and religious division, tended to vote for the Conservative Party. This was because the Conservatives supported the union between Ireland and Britain. The Orange Order had some political influence, with some MPs in the 1920s and 1930s being involved in the order. Sir John Gilmour, Secretary of State for Scotland (1924–9), is one example.

Activity 1

Summarise this chapter

The following summary reminds you of what this chapter has been about. Words that are important have been made into ANAGRAMS. Your task is to sort out the anagrams and then write the correct version of this summary into your workbook or work file.

In the nineteenth century, Irish **SAMMITRING** came to Scotland in large numbers. They came to work in the **ALOC** and **RINO** industries as well as to work as **VIVASEN** on the railways. They made an important contribution to Scotland's **CONEYOM**. Irish immigrants lived in the poorer areas of Glasgow, **REBIDHUNG** and **DUDEEN**. Relations between the Scottish and the Irish people varied. Many Scottish people saw the **ALTOCHIC** Irish as a threat, but the relationship has changed in positive ways. However, there is still **JUICEDPER** against the Irish Catholics. The **ENTRAPTOTS** Irish got on well with the Scots as they had the same religion. They also brought the **AGONER** Lodge over from Ireland.

Activity 2

If this is the answer, then what is the question?

Below you will find a list of words or phrases. You have to make up a question that can only be answered by the word or phrase on the list. For example, if the word 'navvies' was the answer, a question could be 'What was the name given to the people who built the railways?'

▶ Orange Lodge
▶ Catholic
▶ Sinn Féin
▶ Labour Party
▶ Union
▶ Temperance organisations.

Activity 3

Mapping information

Sketch, copy or download a map of Scotland. Around your map write as many words as you can find that link to the effects of Irish immigration on Scotland.

Now write a short description of the impact of Irish people on Scotland using the help given here. Match the missing words 1–9 with the words a–i below. When you have made your choices, write out the complete paragraph.

Irish people had a large impact on Scotland. This can be seen in the separate [1] schools that developed. It can also be seen in the spread of the [2] Lodge across Scotland. The Irish had a huge impact on the [3] of Scotland. They were important in building the [4] and working in industries like [5]. We can also see their impact through the football clubs that exist in Scotland today. Clubs like [6] and [7] were started by Irish Catholic immigrants. Politically, the Irish were important in the [8] Party before the First World War. After the war, many Irish turned to the [9] Party as they supported workers' rights.

a Labour	d Catholic	g railways
b Orange	e economy	h Liberal
c Celtic	f Hibernian	i coal mining

Question practice

National 4

Source A is about the Irish poor in Scotland.

SOURCE A

The Irish are, in general, dirtier and less well clothed than the native population. In consequence of the crowded nature of Irish lodging houses, typhus is more common among the Irish in Glasgow than among the Scotch.

Describe the living conditions of the Irish people when they settled in Scotland. You should use Source A and your own knowledge.

Success criteria

Include at least two factual points or one developed piece of information on the living conditions of Irish people when they settled in Scotland. These should be key points but may not be connected.

National 5

Source A is from the *Menace of the Irish Race to our Scottish Nationality*, a pamphlet produced by the Church of Scotland, 1923.

SOURCE A

With the industrial development of Scotland in the nineteenth century, demand for cheap labour arose. Industrial firms and great contractors advertised for labour in the Irish press and crowds of Irishmen and their families emigrated to Scotland to engage in building railways, to work in coal mines, in the great shipyards on the Clyde, in the jute mills of Dundee and to labour in the construction of public works, such as the Loch Katrine waterscheme. When they had settled down they invited relations and friends to come across to Scotland promising to find work and give a home to them. All were welcomed by the employers of labour.

How fully does Source A explain the impact of Irish immigrants on Scotland? You should use Source A and your own knowledge. (6 marks)

▶ Place the source in context by explaining information in the source and applying that information to your own knowledge.
▶ A maximum of 2 marks may be given for answers in which no judgement has been made.
▶ Up to 3 marks can be gained for explaining points of information from the source.
▶ Up to 4 marks can be gained for explaining points of information from your own knowledge which are relevant to the question asked.
▶ Pieces of information from your own knowledge can act either as further explanation of points of information from the source or as new points.

Chapter 6 What was life like for Jewish, Lithuanian and Italian immigrants in Scotland?

What is this chapter about?

This chapter looks at the jobs and the types of lives that Jewish, Lithuanian and Italian immigrants had when they came to Scotland. Sometimes, the immigrants did not get a friendly reception from the Scots, but over time their relationship changed. Some groups assimilated into Scottish life better than others.

By the end of this chapter you should be able to:

▸ Describe what it was like for Jewish, Lithuanian and Italian immigrants to live in Scotland.
▸ Describe the sorts of jobs done by Jewish, Lithuanian and Italian immigrants.
▸ Explain why Scots people were not always friendly towards the new immigrants.
▸ Explain how the Jewish, Lithuanian and Italian communities in Scotland assimilated with the Scots.

What were living conditions like for Jewish immigrants?

Most Jewish immigrants lived in the Gorbals area of Glasgow. The Gorbals was a poor area where cheap housing could be rented. Other smaller Jewish communities were located in places like Edinburgh and Dundee.

Living conditions were not good. Monty Berkeley, from a Russian Jewish family that lived in Tolcross, and then later the Gorbals, describes what it was like in the 1920s and 1930s:

The Gorbals had a whole series of streets and you had a great deal of alcoholism, drunkenness, bad lighting in the stairs. They were spiral metal staircases going up. You'd have as many as four tenants on a landing in flats with only one room and kitchen. The worst area was Thistle Street, Hospital Street and Govan Street.

GLOSSARY

Alcoholism compulsive or addictive alcohol drinking

The Jewish community worked hard. As the people became wealthier, the Jewish population moved to better areas of the city. In Glasgow, that meant the south of the city to places like Shawlands, Clarkston and Giffnock.

A street scene in the Gorbals area of Glasgow in about 1850.

Were Jewish immigrants really all that different from Scots?

The Jewish community was very obviously different from the local Scots. They had a different language, called Yiddish, and had a different religion from the Scots. In 1879, the first purpose-built **synagogue** opened in Garnethill in Glasgow.

The presence of large numbers of poor Jews living in Scottish cities led to some anti-Semitic comments in newspapers. In August 1905, the *Daily Record and Mail* in the west of Scotland reported that Britain was too easy for immigrants to get into and Jews were described as an 'alien danger: immigrants infected with loathsome disease'.

The main entrance to Garnethill synagogue in central Glasgow.

Jews were **stereotyped** as talking oddly and lending money with high interest charges. However, anti-Semitism was not common. Most Scots got on reasonably well with Jews. One reason may have been because of the shared experience of living together in poor housing. Murdoch Rogers comments:

It was possibly because they shared in the poverty that surrounded them that there was little active opposition to the Jews at street or tenement/close level. The immigrant Jews in fact lived a fairly self-contained and independent existence, well organised but poor, tolerated but not accepted.

What sorts of jobs did the Jews do?

Jewish immigrants tended to do different jobs from other immigrant groups. At first, many became pedlars or hawkers. That means they were door-to-door salesmen, trying to sell small cheap items that most households could use.

Ralph Glasser remembers:

Loans were granted free mainly to pedlars and travellers. That gave them the basis for making a living from the stock that they could buy and sell. They were selling various things, braces, mouth-organs, games, small things that needed small money for stock.

Once the door-to-door sellers had made some money they tended to open small shops. Mrs Aitken remembers about the shops that they ran:

It was nearly all Jewish shops and Jewish firms in the Gorbals. There was the Fogels, the corner of Hospital Street and Cleland Street, there was the Jewish bakery at the corner of Dunmore Street. They all opened little shops, just doing alterations and repairs to suits and everything. It was a great place, the Gorbals.

The Jewish community worked hard, often in jobs that had long hours, low pay and bad conditions. Often these jobs involved making clothes. Work involving low pay and long hours was called sweated industry and the workers were known as sweaters who worked in sweatshops. Many workers in sweated trades were Jewish immigrants.

Trade unions were against sweated labour as it reduced the wages of their members. Jewish immigrants were blamed for reducing wages in the industries they worked in. A tailors' trade union leader claimed to the 1899 House of Lords Select Committee on Sweating that:

The wholesale sweaters in Glasgow are chiefly Jews and the number is said to be increasing, though on this point evidence is somewhat scanty. It is computed that the workers in the tailoring trade in Glasgow number about 5000 or 6000.

Were Jewish immigrants treated badly by Scots?

The Jewish population was never very large in Scotland but in some areas there was resentment of the newcomers. At school during the Second World War, Alex Bernstein remembered being bullied for being different:

When I went to school I was the only Jewish kid in class, in fact I was the only Jewish kid in school. And at that time, during the war, I was knocked around like hell. The kids used to crowd around me, pinch my pieces from me and shout 'You German Jew, you German Jew' (even though I was of Russian descent). As a result my life was hell there. It made me a very timid child.

On the other hand, life seemed to get better for Alex:

I lived, up until I was 14, in Stockwell Street, which is just over the bridge from the Gorbals, and there it was a wee mini Gorbals. There was quite a number of families, Jewish families and the kids used to play together and we used to play with the non-Jewish kids as well …

Jewish kids and the Protestant kids used to band together in the 'billy' or the 'dandy'. You know when you are challenged in the street 'Are you a billy or a dan or are you an old tin can?' If you were a billy, you were a Protestant and you got a hammering from a Catholic, if you were a dan you got a hammering from a Protestant, but if you were an old tin can you were a Jew and you were more or less safe.

How important was Jewish Immigration to the economic growth of Scotland?

One important impact of the Jewish community was the creation of a new industry in Scotland. There was no local workforce that could produce cigarettes. The Imperial Tobacco Company in Glasgow recruited Jewish tobacco workers from Hamburg in Germany and Warsaw in Poland. Cigarette making was a common job for the Jewish immigrants to Scotland.

The success of Glasgow tobacco production attracted other tobacco manufacturers to Glasgow. The Jewish population also contributed to the economy of Scotland with their work in the production of clothes.

> How can you tell that the shop is owned by a Jewish person?

Abraham Links' drapery shop in Main Street in the Gorbals, 1907.

Lithuanians in Scotland

Lithuanian immigrants arrived in Scotland in the late nineteenth century and worked in the growing industries of coal, iron and steel in Lanarkshire and Ayrshire.

What were living conditions like for Lithuanian immigrants?

Like the Irish, the Lithuanian community in Scotland was visibly different from the local Scots. They spoke a different language and were Catholic. They also tended to live together in the streets of the Scottish towns where they settled.

Matt Mitchell remembers one street in the village of Carfin, near Motherwell:

I can still repeat the Lithuanian names. First house: Yafortskus, Baukauskus, Kvdera, Curzeatis, Lizdus and Koshinsky. That was the first building in Carfin coming from New Stevenston. It was totally Lithuanian and the other side was nearly the same.

Were Lithuanian immigrants really all that different from Scots?

For a time, in places like Wishaw, the Lithuanians developed their own communities. However, the Lithuanian community was small compared with the Irish one. Lithuanians were eventually absorbed into the local community. One reason is because Lithuanian identity was lost when names were changed. Employers found their names difficult to say, so changed them. In this way, for example, Kanapinskas became Kane and Bernotatitis became Smith.

There is some evidence of racist attitudes with Lithuanian children picked on as being 'dirty Poles'. Lithuanian children went to local schools as there were not enough of them to have separate schools. However, the Lithuanian community fairly quickly lost its own identity. Many Lithuanians gave up their old surnames and intermarriage between Lithuanians and Scots became more common. Lithuanians went to Scottish schools so speaking English became normal. The old Lithuanian language was eventually forgotten in Scotland.

Were Lithuanian immigrants treated badly by Scots?

Like the Catholic Irish, the Lithuanians were treated badly when they first arrived in Scottish communities. The Lithuanian miners were used to break strikes and were willing to work for less money than the Scots. This led to fighting between Scottish and Lithuanian workers, but soon Lithuanians joined with Scots in campaigning for better pay and conditions.

Italians in Scotland

Italians started to arrive in Scotland from the 1890s onwards. Most of the Italian immigrants were trying to escape hunger and poverty back home in Italy. By 1914, the Italian community in Scotland numbered about 4500. Italian families were spread out across Scotland.

This photograph shows an Italian 'hokey pokey' seller in 1898 in a Scottish city. He has covered his ornate and beautiful cart with a striped and fringed awning. 'Hokey pokey' was slang for ice-cream in Scotland at the time.

Did Scots and Italians get on?

There was opposition to Italian businesses from some Scots. Many Italian cafés, ice-cream shops and fish and chip shops opened on a Sunday. This was opposed by people who thought that Sunday should be kept as a **sabbath**. Other Scots liked the cafés because they did not serve alcohol. Young people liked them because they were a place to meet and socialise.

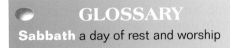

GLOSSARY

Sabbath a day of rest and worship

Were Italian immigrants really all that different from Scots?

The Italian community in Scotland worked hard. The long hours of work meant that they did not always integrate with the local Scottish population. Joe Pieri remembered:

The counter between myself and our customers acted as a barrier. We were aliens, foreigners, the Tallies [slang for Italians] who worked all day to serve them fish and chips and ice-cream, and we were tolerated as such.

Nardini's café and ice-cream parlour in Largs was originally opened in 1935. It shows the kind of business that many Italian immigrants set up.

Italian families also wanted to make enough money to return to Italy. Intermarriage or even dating between Italians and Scots was not approved of.

Mrs Lucchesi was a young girl in 1914:

My father wanted us to be as much Italian as we possibly could. Food at home was Italian, we spoke Italian, we had Italian friends and we were brought up that we had to marry Italians. It wasn't only our family for that was a general thing with the Italians. The social life, especially for the girls, was very restricted. We got on very well with the Scots boys who came into the shop and would chat with us, but then they stopped asking us out because they knew we wouldn't go out. It was forbidden.

What sorts of jobs did the Italians do?

Most Italians found work in family businesses such as cafés, fish and chip shops and ice-cream parlours.

Joe Pieri remembers:

The ice-cream shops that developed from the ice-cream barrows once pushed through the streets by Italian immigrants added a new dimension to the leisure life of the youth of Scotland. The shops stayed open late and provided them with a place to meet. Fish and chip shops matched the growth of the cafés and provided the working classes with a cheap and nourishing meal which grew to be a part of their diet.

Did immigrants help the economic development of Scotland?

Immigrants contributed to the economic development of Scotland. Some immigrants, like the Lithuanians, helped in the heavy industries while Jews were more involved in commercial activities. Other groups, like the Italians, brought new jobs and skills that added to Scotland's culture.

Activity 1

Graffiti board

Choose a part of your classroom to be dedicated as a graffiti board where you can write and record your thoughts on the issues raised by the relationship between Scots and immigrants.

You might be asked to contribute to the graffiti board at different times using the K-W-L technique:

▷ **Know**: what do you know about the different relationships between Scots and immigrants?
▷ **Want**: what do you want to know about the relationship?
▷ **Learned**: what have you learned at the end of the topic?

After class discussions, new comments can also be added to the graffiti board. You should feel free to contribute to the graffiti board at any time during the course of a topic.

Activity 2

Summarise this chapter

The following summary reminds you of what this chapter has been about. Words that are important in this chapter have been made into ANAGRAMS. Your task is to sort out the anagrams then write the correct version of this summary into your workbook or work file.

Jewish, Lithuanian and Italian immigrants came to live and work in Scotland. They had different experiences when they came here. Jewish people did some jobs that Scots did not do. They worked as **HARKSEW** and **RASPLED** selling useful items door to door. They also worked in **SEATWED** industries. These were low-paid jobs. The **ACOBCOT** and **GLITCHNO** industries developed because of Jewish immigrants. Lithuanian immigrants worked in the **LCAO** and **ORNI** industries in central Scotland. The Italians added to Scotland's culture by opening ice-cream **ALSOPURR** and **SIHF** and **HCPI** shops.

Jewish immigrants generally got on well with Scots, but there was some **TNAI-ICEMIST** feeling from some people. Jews kept their own culture and **IRELINGO**. The Lithuanians lived together and were used to break **TREKSIS** to begin with. However, they joined **TADRE SIONUN** and worked together with Scots. Lithuanians eventually **STADIALIMES** well with Scots through marriage and changing their names. The Italian community remained **PARASTEE** from Scots due to the long hours their jobs needed.

Question practice

National 4

Source A is about Lithuanian immigrants in Scotland.

SOURCE A

Many Lithuanian immigrants to Scotland came from the countryside. They learned to work in the coal industry. Both men and women worked hard. Lithuanian women could be found working on the surface of the coal mines, while their men worked underground.

Describe the impact of immigrants on the Scottish economy. You should use Source A and your own knowledge.

Success criteria

Write at least two factual points of information or one developed piece of information about the impact of immigrants on the Scottish economy.

National 5

Source A is a personal account of life in Scotland by a Scottish-Italian woman called Mrs Lucchesi. She is writing about life before 1914.

SOURCE A

My father wanted us to be as much Italian as we possibly could. Food at home was Italian, we spoke Italian, we had Italian friends and we were brought up that we had to marry Italians. It wasn't only our family for that was a general thing with the Italians. The social life, especially for the girls, was very restricted. We got on very well with the Scots boys who came into the shop and would chat with us, but then they stopped asking us out because they knew we wouldn't go out. It was forbidden.

1 Evaluate the usefulness of Source A as evidence of the relationship between Italian immigrants and Scots. You may want to comment on who wrote it, when they wrote it, why they wrote it and what they say or what has been missed out. **(6 marks)**

Success criteria

- To get 1 mark, you need to explain the importance of each of the points you make about the source.
- Up to 4 marks may be given for evaluative comments about origin and purpose. Comments about the origin may include an explanation about the type of source, the author or the timing of the source. Comments about purpose may include an explanation about why the source was written.
- Up to 2 marks may be given for your evaluation of the content of the source which you consider is useful in terms of the proposed question. For full marks to be given, each point needs to be discretely mentioned and its usefulness explained. If you list information, that will be considered to be one point and will get only 1 mark.
- Up to 2 marks may be given for evaluative comments relating to points of information not mentioned in the source.

Source B is from Ben Braber's book *Jews in Glasgow 1879–1939*, published in 2007.

SOURCE B

Jewish immigrants usually lacked the skills and contacts to take up positions in heavy industry. However, they were able to supply the local industry and its employees with goods and services. For example, Abraham Goldberg brought his first bale of cloth in 1900 and took it to his room-and-kitchen home in the Gorbals to turn it into goods for sale to wholesalers. It was the start of a multi-million pound business. At the same time other Jews in Glasgow were occupied in similar, though smaller, enterprises. One Buchanan Street business was tobacconist Morris Cohen. Morris was the founder of J. Cohen and Sons, described as, 'importers of cigars, pipe manufacturers, and fancy good merchants'.

Source C is from historian Tom Devine's book called *The Scottish Nation*, published in 1999.

SOURCE C

The Jewish immigrant economy was remarkably self-contained. The majority ran or worked in Jewish-owned businesses as tailors, cigarette makers, tobacconists, hawkers, pedlars and travellers. Jews possessed skills developed in the urban economy in Europe which they were able to utilise when they settled in Glasgow. There was no real wish, therefore, despite their poverty, to compete alongside the Irish and the Lithuanians for work in the docks, mines and steel mills.

2 Compare the views of Sources B and C about the employment of Jewish immigrants in Scotland. **(4 marks)**

This is a 'source comparison' question. You need to compare what the sources say about the issue on a 'point-by-point' basis.

Success criteria

- You should interpret evidence from the sources.
- You should include direct comparisons between the information in the sources.
- You can get up to 4 marks for making four simple comparisons between the information in the two sources.
- You can get up to 4 marks for making two developed comparisons between the two sources.
- A simple comparison: 'Source B says … and Source C says …' will get 1 mark.
- A developed comparison: 'Sources B and C agree about the fact that Jews did not work in heavy industry. Source B says … and Source C says …' will get 2 marks.

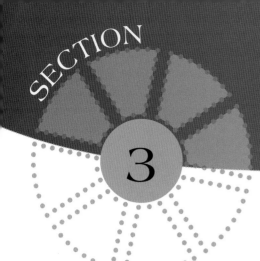

Scottish emigration, 1830s–1939

Chapter 7 Why did problems in Scotland encourage Scots to emigrate?

What is this chapter about?

Throughout history, Scots have had a tradition of moving abroad because of a lack of jobs and opportunities within Scotland. Changing ways of working on the land meant that fewer people were needed in Scottish agriculture. Scotland was also a low-wage economy. Lack of opportunities in Scotland to improve people's lives led many of them to leave.

By the end of this chapter you should be able to:

▶ Describe the problems that led to emigration from Scotland.
▶ Explain why poverty and lack of opportunity led Scots to emigrate.

Why did Scots move abroad?

Some Scots were forced to emigrate. They had to go because of poverty or unemployment. There was no future for their families if they stayed in Scotland. Historians call these reasons push factors.

> **GLOSSARY**
>
> **Agricultural depression**
> a downturn in the money made from land and fishing from 1880 to 1914

In the nineteenth century, the experience of emigration was very different between the Highlands and the Lowlands. Often, people from the Highlands had no choice but to move. In the Lowlands, people were more likely to move because they wanted a better standard of living. After 1860, most Scots left because of a lack of opportunities at home.

Poverty and homelessness were the main reasons people were forced to emigrate. However, the causes of homelessness and poverty were different depending on whether a person lived in the Highlands or the Lowlands. Another reason for emigration was the impact of the **agricultural depression** that affected Scotland from 1880 until 1914. After the First World War, economic problems and lack of opportunities led Scots people to emigrate in large numbers again.

Why did Scots leave the Highlands?

People in the Highlands were badly affected by rising costs. Rents rose quickly and became too high for many. There were also a series of crop failures that meant people went hungry or did not have surplus crops to sell to raise money to pay their rents. Added to this, landowners wanted to develop grouse shooting and deer hunting on their estates so they encouraged people to emigrate who were poor and no longer useful to them. In some cases, landowners even paid the fares and costs for local people to emigrate.

Highlanders were also evicted from their homes, usually to places on the coast at first. Although forced eviction was not the most common reason for people emigrating from the Highlands, the fear that it might happen added to the misery of Highlanders.

Duncan Shaw, a **land factor** for Harris and North Uist, described to a parliamentary committee in 1841 what happened to Highlanders who were **cleared** from a farm so that it could be rented to a single sheep farmer:

Three years were allowed for them to prepare. They were told they must leave by Easter 1839. Those of them who were unfit for emigration were offered better lands elsewhere in Harris. Those able to emigrate were told that their whole rent arrears would be dropped and that they and their families would be landed in Cape Breton, Canada, free of expense.

The main regions of Scotland from which people emigrated.

> ## GLOSSARY
>
> **Land factor** a landlord's agent who collects rent and deals with tenants
>
> **Cleared** a way of saying 'evicted' or 'removed' that doesn't sound so bad
>
> **Clearances** the eviction and removal of a large number of Highland farmers

Were landowners really as unfair as some people have claimed?

Forced evictions or **clearances** were at their height in the 1840s and early 1850s. After 1855, there were no large-scale clearances. Landlords were heavily criticised by some commentators at the time of the clearances. Men like Alexander Mackenzie opposed emigration as they believed it was destroying an ancient way of life and preventing land reform which would allow more people to stay. Other commentators like Donald Macleod and Donald Ross gave first-hand accounts of alleged landlord atrocities and claimed that Highlanders were forced to emigrate because landlords had been greedy. Macleod and Ross said that there were more than enough resources to support the population in the Highlands if they had been shared out

How do you think the people in the photograph are feeling?

An evicted family in Lochmaddy, Harris in 1895.

properly. Donald Macleod believed that emigration had disastrous consequences for the Highlanders. He described what happened at Red River colony. This was a colony set up in what is now on the Canadian/US border by Lord Selkirk to give some evicted Highland farmers a new start:

They were without any protection from the hoards of Red Indian savages by whom the district was infested and who plundered them of their all on their arrival and finally massacred them.

What evidence is there that the people being evicted are being forced to do so?

An eviction in Argyll around 1880–1900.

Some historians believe that the anti-emigration campaign did not give the whole picture of why Highlanders emigrated. They say that the claims of poor conditions of Highlanders in places like Canada were found to be untrue. Also, they claimed that the campaign ignored the fact that Highlanders took the initiative in escaping suffering and poverty. They chose destinations like Canada because the quality of land and opportunities contrasted with the poor living to be made from crofts in places like the Hebrides, where the failure of the kelp industry had created further poverty for Highlanders.

What other agricultural developments caused Scots to emigrate?

Throughout the nineteenth century, many people emigrated from farming areas in the Lowlands of Scotland. This was because scientific improvements and new machines were being used to produce more food, leading to a fall in the number of workers needed. Another change that led to people being forced to leave was the growing specialisation in farming. Different areas of Scotland started to concentrate on a specific product, for example, dairy products in the south-west or grain in East Lothian. Specialisation tended to lead to bigger farms, which meant that it was harder for young farmworkers to get the money or experience to set up their own farms. There was a growing division in the status between farmers and labourers because of low wages and the lack of chances for farmworkers to improve their lives. Lack of opportunity was a major reason for emigration from the Lowlands.

How did the agricultural depression cause emigration from Scotland?

Agricultural depression caused emigration from about 1880 to 1914. Several reasons led to the depression. These included low grain prices, high rents and wet weather which meant that many farmworkers decided to cut their losses and move abroad. The growing use of machinery such as tractors meant that fewer workers were needed. Housing in rural areas was often very poor so that there was no incentive to remain on the land. Another reason was the attraction of moving to the towns where wages were higher and there was at least the possibility of an improvement in life chances. Once people had moved to the towns, it was much easier for them to think about moving again – this time to another country.

Fishing also suffered a depression from about 1884 to 1894. It led to significant emigration from coastal towns that made their money from this industry. People working in fishing communities were often related in some way. People from these communities were more likely to emigrate in family groups because they worked in the same trade. Emigration was a difficult decision and was only considered as a last resort. An upturn in the industry in the years before the First World War led to a drop in the number of people emigrating.

Why did prisoners increase emigration?

Up until 1867, prisoners convicted of serious crimes were often sent to Australia. Sentences could last from seven years to life depending on the crime. About 7600 Scottish convicts were sent to Australia in this way. After serving their sentences many ex-convicts chose to stay in Australia. Sometimes, their families moved from Scotland to join them.

What problems after the First World War led to more emigration?

In 1923, 88,584 people emigrated from Scotland. In fact, so many Scots left that the population actually decreased in the 1920s despite over 350,000 Scots being born! The Highlands lost the largest number of people, closely followed by the far north. Lowland agricultural areas also lost people. The 1920s is the only period of history where the population of Scotland has decreased between **census** records.

> **GLOSSARY**
> **Census** a count of the population organised by the government every ten years

> How can you tell that these emigrants are happy to be leaving Scotland?

WE`VE GOT JOBS IN CANADA WE DON`T WANT THE DOLE!

A group of Scottish emigrants on board a ship on their way to Canada in 1925.

The reasons for emigration are complicated but closely linked to the economic problems that Scotland experienced after the First World War. After a short post-war boom, Scotland struggled to get foreign orders. The country depended on industries such as shipbuilding, engineering, steel and coal but these struggled with increasing foreign competition. Many Scots who left in the 1920s were young and well educated; they left because of a lack of opportunities at home. Increasing foreign competition also affected the fishing industry after the First World War. As a result, the fishing industry lost valuable overseas markets, such as Russia, and the Highlanders lost much-needed part-time earnings. This was one reason why emigration from some areas was so high. In the Lowlands, the increasing use of machines and cheap food imports caused more people to leave.

Scots also left because countries like the USA started to limit the number of people allowed into the country. One reason why Scottish emigration was so high in 1923 was because people chose to emigrate before the limits took effect.

Margaret Kirk emigrated from Scotland to the USA in 1923 and the reasons she gave for leaving were typical of many Scots people:

There was loads of work while the [First World] war was on. As soon as the war finished, everybody was getting laid off. There was a depression in the country, and everybody wanted to come to America. There was nothing, there was no work, so they were gasping for a job. And America sent out signals that everything was wonderful here, so they came to America.

Why did Scots continue to emigrate in the 1930s?

Scots continued to emigrate in the 1930s but in much smaller numbers. People continued to leave because the traditional industries were still doing badly. It is estimated that unemployment was 50 per cent higher in Scotland than in England. There was little government help for those areas of Scotland, such as the Clydeside area, which experienced the greatest hardship. For example, there was just one government job training centre in Springburn, Glasgow, which could train only about 500 men a year. Most Scots workers who got on the government scheme had to go to England to take up a place.

Not only were Scotland's traditional industries doing badly, but Scotland failed to develop new enterprises. The number of jobs being created was only half that of England, and Scotland's share of industrial production and national income also fell. Once again, the lack of opportunities pushed Scots to emigrate.

Activity 1

Building a learning wall

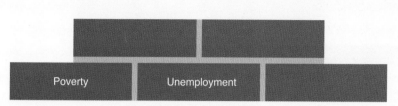

Poverty   Unemployment

Create your own learning wall on why Scots were forced to emigrate.

Work in pairs or small groups. Each group should write down on a piece of paper or a Post-it note their ideas about why Scots were forced to emigrate. Each reason should be on a separate piece of paper or note.

Each group should use their reasons to 'construct' their learning wall. You should work through the reasons, deciding as a group on how relevant each reason is. Each group should then place the important reasons on the bottom line of the wall and the least important factors at the top.

Groups should then give feedback on their decisions, justifying their choices if they are different from those of another group. Your teacher might ask you to peer assess each other's work.

Activity 2

Creating a fish-bone diagram

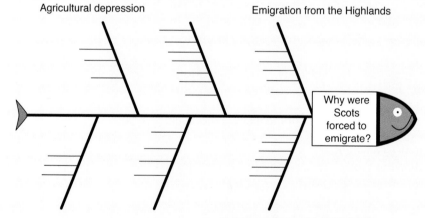

Agricultural depression

Emigration from the Highlands

Why were Scots forced to emigrate?

Problems after the First World War

You should work in small groups to produce a fish-bone diagram. Your teacher will give you a template with the key question: 'Why were Scots forced to emigrate?' The template will give you the outline of a fish skeleton.

Each group should place 'Why were Scots forced to emigrate?' at the front of the skeleton. The main fish bones represent possible main causes. The smaller horizontal bones add further detail to the main bones. Some of the main causes have already been filled in.

Question practice

National 4

Source A is from Margaret Kirk, who emigrated to the USA in 1923 at the age of 22.

SOURCE A

There was loads of work while the [First World] war was on. As soon as the war finished, everybody was getting laid off. There was a depression in the country, and everybody wanted to come to America. There was nothing, there was no work, so they were gasping for a job. And America sent out signals that everything was wonderful here, so they came to America.

Explain why Scots were forced to emigrate from Scotland. You should use Source A and your own knowledge.

Success criteria

Explain in your own words what Source A tells you about why Scots decided to emigrate.

National 5

Explain why Scots were forced to emigrate from Scotland. **(5 marks)**

This is an 'explain' question. That means you must give five reasons why something did or did not happen. It is not enough just to write down facts, no matter how correct they are. You must make clear exactly how these facts did or did not allow something to happen. In terms of this question, your writing must use facts to show why Scots were forced to emigrate from Scotland.

There will not be a source in the exam to help you, but to get you started on your answer here are some hints:

- Explain the reasons for emigration from the Highlands. (This could give you more than one reason for emigration.)
- Explain why Scots emigrated from the Lowlands.
- Explain how the agricultural depression caused Scots to leave. (This could give you more than one reason for emigration.)
- Explain how crime caused Scots to emigrate.
- Explain how problems after the First World War caused Scots to emigrate. (This could give you more than one reason for emigration.)

Success criteria

- 1 mark to be given for each relevant point of information. A second mark can be given for any reason that is developed.
- Include at least five or six reasons why Scots were forced to emigrate.
- Give accurate and detailed pieces of information that are properly explained.

Chapter 8 What attracted Scots to emigrate abroad?

What is this chapter about?

The attractions of living abroad made many Scots want to move. These are called pull factors. Some attractions were practical, such as cheap and quick transport links. Other people emigrated from Scotland because of the prospects that existed abroad. These opportunities included the chance to earn more money and have a better quality of life.

By the end of this chapter you should be able to:

▶ Describe the developments and organisations that attracted Scots to move abroad.
▶ Explain the reasons why Scots wanted to emigrate.

Why did improvements in transport help Scots to emigrate?

During the nineteenth century it became easier for ordinary Scots to travel overseas to find new work opportunities. People emigrated because they could do so easily and cheaply. The invention of the steamship reduced the time and risk of sailing to a new country. In 1850, the journey across the Atlantic took six weeks, but in 1914 the journey time had fallen to around a week.

Scots also benefited from the building of the railways, which meant that they could easily get to the ports where the ships departed. From the 1850s, Scottish emigrants had an advantage: Clyde shipping firms developed a network of worldwide services that enabled passengers to book travel to final destinations abroad.

How did emigration societies help Scots to leave?

Emigration was expensive. Money was needed to help pay for the travel costs and for building new homes abroad, for example. Many Scots needed financial help to move. There were various sources of money to help people emigrate:

▶ landowners
▶ government money
▶ charities
▶ emigration societies
▶ colonial governments.

Estate landowners helped with the costs of emigration because they wanted to reduce the number of people living on their lands. Some landlords were genuinely trying to help but others were more selfish. Some landlords wanted to get rid of workers who might soon become unable to work and would therefore want help from their landlord or, worse still, might be unable to pay the rent.

Landlords also sometimes helped by negotiating for land, on behalf of their tenants, with the government of countries like Canada. Landowners like Lord Selkirk and the Duke of Hamilton gave their tenants considerable help.

However, some landlords like Colonel Gordon were more ruthless. He evicted 1770 people from his estates in South Uist, Barra and Benbecula but failed to fund their passage to Canada properly. This caused outrage at home in Scotland and in Canada.

How did the government help emigrants?

The government did very little to help emigrants in the nineteenth century, apart from in the 1880s when it gave £10,000 to help Highland crofters to emigrate. More help was given after the First World War. That was because the government now saw emigration as way of dealing with the growing unemployment problem.

The government set up the Overseas Settlement Committee, which began to try to settle ex-servicemen overseas. However, the scheme only lasted until 1923 and helped less than a third of those who had applied. In 1922, the government passed the Empire Settlement Act, which gave £3 million a year to help with travel expenses, training and the buying of land. But by 1937, this amount was halved. That was because countries who had accepted emigrants were no longer as keen because they had their own problems.

Why did charities help Scots to emigrate?

Some better-off people organised help for emigration. Charities like Barnardos did some work in Scotland. Also, the Young Men's Christian Association (YMCA) sent men to the former colonies between the First and Second World Wars. The British Women's Emigration Association did the same job for young women. One of the best-known individuals was William Quarrier. He made a fortune from a boot and shoe business after having a poor upbringing in the Gorbals, Glasgow. He set up children's homes for orphans. From 1872, he began sending some children from his homes to new lives in Canada. By 1933, when the scheme ended, he had sent nearly 7000 children.

What did emigration societies do?

The early emigration societies were concentrated in the west of Scotland, mainly in Lanarkshire and Renfrewshire. They helped people like weavers who were finding it harder to make a living with growing competition from machines in factories. The societies usually tried to get government money to help families to emigrate, with varying success.

> **GLOSSARY**
>
> **Weavers** people who make fabrics from fibres

Emigration societies also helped women. Towards the end of the nineteenth century, the government realised that more women had to emigrate in order to balance the population in the former colonies. For example, in 1850, 19 Shetland women (where there were three for every man) were sent to Australia. One of the best-known Scottish female emigration societies was the Aberdeen Ladies' Union, which sent 330 women to Canada between 1883 and 1914.

Why did colonial governments help Scottish emigrants?

The governments which ruled the different parts of the British Empire put a lot of effort into attracting certain people. Places like Canada hoped to attract well-qualified farmers and workers to help develop their economy. They continued to do so until the mid 1930s when economic problems of their own meant that they no longer wanted new immigrants.

To persuade Scots people to emigrate, colonial governments tried to convince them that they would be better off by emigrating. Most colonial governments had offices in Scotland and regularly gave talks and handed out leaflets advertising the attractiveness of the new lands. Countries like Canada and the USA had great success in attracting well-educated and able Scots workers.

Identify how each poster is trying to tempt Scots to emigrate.

Canadian posters trying to attract emigrants.

In the later nineteenth century, there was an explosion in the quality and quantity of information available to potential emigrants. In 1892, the Canadian government appointed two full-time agents in Scotland who undertook tours of markets, hiring fairs, agricultural shows and village halls. From the 1870s to the Great War, the Canadian government aimed to settle the Prairie West with farmers. The rural districts of Scotland were especially targeted because of their historic links with Canada and the country's reputation for experienced farmers and skilled agricultural workers.

T.M. Devine, To the Ends of the Earth: Scotland's Global Diaspora, 1750–2010, published in 2011

How effective was the support for emigration?

There has been debate about the value of support for emigration for several reasons:

- There were many different societies and schemes which duplicated each others' efforts.
- Government support was not reliable until after the First World War.
- The number of people that were helped was fairly small compared to the total number of emigrants.
- Government support for emigration was often not motivated by genuine concern. For example, the support for female emigration in the late nineteenth century was more about benefiting the government policy rather than helping women.
- Often the poorest were not helped by government support. Sometimes this was because colonial governments preferred people with education and skills but also because poorer people lacked the ability to **lobby** the right people for their cause.

In 1844, Archibald Alison, Sheriff Deputy of Lanarkshire, talked about why he had some 30–40 weaver emigration societies from Glasgow applying for help but virtually none from Paisley:

I suspect that the persons from the Glasgow societies are not in total poverty and therefore have spirit enough to bear the idea of a transatlantic voyage. But in Paisley, they are in such a state of poverty and depression, that the very idea of moving is horrible. I have seen cases where people would have willingly emigrated but when they had sunk into deep poverty would not.

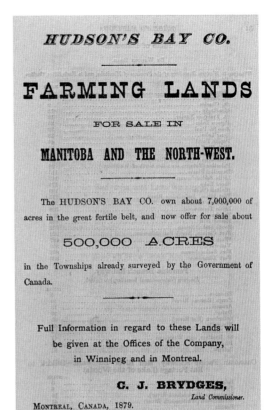

HUDSON'S BAY CO.

FARMING LANDS

FOR SALE IN

MANITOBA AND THE NORTH-WEST.

The HUDSON'S BAY CO. own about 7,000,000 of acres in the great fertile belt, and now offer for sale about

500,000 ACRES

in the Townships already surveyed by the Government of Canada.

Full Information in regard to these Lands will be given at the Offices of the Company, in Winnipeg and in Montreal.

C. J. BRYDGES,
Land Commissioner.

MONTREAL, CANADA, 1879.

A leaflet offering farmland for sale to Scottish emigrants.

GLOSSARY

Lobby to influence government officials to change a policy

Missionaries members of religious groups who travel away from home in order to try and spread their faith's message more widely

Why did religion encourage some Scots to emigrate?

The British Empire contained many different peoples with different religious beliefs. Some men and women in Scotland believed that it was their Christian duty to convert the people of the Empire to Christianity. Many of the **missionaries** took practical skills as well as their faith. For example, Alexander Duff set up the Madras College in India and Dr Jane Waterson set up a girls' school in South Africa, working as a doctor and a missionary in Nyasaland. One of the best-known missionaries was David Livingstone, who went to Africa. Livingstone is a good example of how Church work offered opportunities for Scots abroad. He started his working life in a cotton mill at the age of ten. However, thanks to the education he received, which was funded by the Church, Livingstone went on to become a doctor and explorer. He became one of the most famous Scots in history.

What opportunities did living abroad offer to Scots?

> Why might the chance to live in such a house encourage people to emigrate? Think about living conditions in Scotland at the time.

A house in the late nineteenth century that was used to attract emigrants to Canada.

The big attraction of emigration for Scottish farmers was the possibility of living in greater comfort and independence – and on their own land. The advantage of Canada was that it was possible to buy land at fair prices without having to go through land companies. Laws passed in 1841 and 1872 regulated the sale and registration of land. Canadian land ownership was promoted in the press as a result.

This is a review of a guidebook on Canada in *Chambers' Edinburgh Journal*:

Just fancy yourselves possessed of real property – no yearly tenancy – no rent to pay. And only think of the advantage of working a rich soil that will yield greatly, instead of ploughing or digging a worn-out one at home that will not yield a crop sufficient to pay for working it.

The USA and New Zealand also offered cheaper, fertile land to farmers.

An advertisement showing the link between Scotland and the land of Canada. Scottish farmers were attractive to countries like Canada as they were skilled.

THE

SCOTTISH CANADIAN LAND & SETTLEMENT ASSOCIATION,

LIMITED.

To be Incorporated under the Companies Acts, 1862 to 1883.

CAPITAL, £500,000

In 50,000 Shares of £10 each, of which 10,000 Shares have been applied for in Canada, and are accordingly reserved. The remaining 40,000 Shares are now offered for Subscription.

Payable as follows:—£1 on Application; £2 on Allotment; £2 when Purchase Price of Lands is payable.

No further Calls are anticipated, as £5 per Share, with borrowing powers, is considered amply sufficient.

PROVISIONAL COMMITTEE.

THE EARL OF MAR AND KELLIE.
SIR REGINALD CATHCART, of Carlton, Bart.
THE HON. DONALD A. SMITH, of Montreal and Silver Heights, Manitoba (Director, Hudson's Bay Company, &c.)
GEORGE STEPHEN, Esq., of Montreal (President, Canadian Pacific Railway).
MACLEOD OF MACLEOD.
DUNCAN FORBES, Esq., of Culloden.
DUNCAN DARROCH, Esq., of Gourock and Torridon.

ALEXANDER HENDERSON, Esq., of Stemster, Convener of County of Caithness.
ALEXANDER ALLAN, Esq. (Messrs. James & Alexander Allan, of the Allan Line), Glasgow.
J. T. GIBSON-CRAIG, Esq., F.R.S.E., W.S., Edinburgh.
REV. JAMES MACGREGOR, D.D., of St. Cuthbert's, Edinburgh.
WILLIAM FORBES SKENE, Esq., D.C.L., LL.D., W.S., Edinburgh.

BANKERS.

IN SCOTLAND:
THE COMMERCIAL BANK OF SCOTLAND (LIMITED) and Branches.

IN CANADA:
THE BANK OF MONTREAL.

SOLICITORS.

SKENE, EDWARDS, & BILTON, W.S., 21 Hill Street, Edinburgh.

INTERIM OFFICE—21 HILL STREET, EDINBURGH.

PROSPECTUS.

THE leading objects of this Association are:—

1. To acquire by purchase, for the purpose of re-sale, 500,000 acres (more or less) of land in Southern Manitoba, and Assiniboia in the Dominion of Canada.

How important were family connections in encouraging Scots to emigrate?

Money and connections were other reasons why Scots emigrated, and why they chose the destinations they did. It was not just the family and community support that was important, relatives often provided money or paid for tickets and gave help to emigrants when they first arrived.

Some Scots were attracted to emigration because of the major investment opportunities that were offered abroad. In other words, they wanted the chance to make a lot of money. Many Scots settled in New Zealand's South Island to farm sheep. Some of the investors came straight from Scotland but others had gained experience in sheep farming in Australia first. Scottish farmers became respected for their abilities in this industry. One of the best-known sheep farming families in Australia were the Leslies, who were originally from Old Rayne in Aberdeenshire.

Scots also invested in North America. Andrew Little from Moffat emigrated in 1894 and became known as the 'sheep king of Idaho'. Scottish investors also set up cattle firms. Not all investment was in land. Scots also put money and engineering expertise into mining and railways. Andrew Carnegie made a vast fortune from providing steel for the railways. Two Scottish cousins, George Stephen from Dufftown and Donald Smith from Forres, funded the building of the Canadian Pacific Railway.

What were the jobs that attracted Scots to emigrate?

Some of the best-known stories about emigration are about people emigrating from rural areas. However, most people who emigrated came from the towns. They did so because they had the education and training to seek a better life abroad. Such workers were mostly craftspeople. Scots made a significant contribution to the textile industry of New England in the USA. In the 1870s, Andover, Massachusetts, became known as a 'second Brechin' after two Angus emigrants set up a linen factory there. The US jute industry was dominated by a group of Dundee emigrants who set up a factory in 1844. The textile industry attracted women as well as men. Many Scottish workers ended up as supervisors, managers and even owners of mills.

The textile industry was only one of many industries that tried to attract Scottish workers. Industries like steel and shipbuilding also had need of more workers. Newspapers and journals contained many job adverts.

In 1870, 46 per cent of all Scots who emigrated to the USA worked in factories, engineering and mining jobs. Many Scottish miners went to Ohio and Illinois in the 1860s, attracted by the high wages that could be earned during the US Civil War.

Did fellow Scots abroad encourage emigration?

Better wages were not the only reason Scots continued to emigrate in large numbers to the same places. The communities created by families and friends were also important. Places were named after the people who emigrated there, such as Bon Accord, Ontario, in Canada which was settled by people from Aberdeenshire. This encouraged even more Scots to emigrate. Guides were published that tried to exploit emigrant concerns about keeping their language and culture. A good example of this is the Gaelic language *Cuairtear nan Gleann*, which was published in Canada in the early 1840s.

Many Scots were attracted to Otago, New Zealand, because it was developed by the Free Church of Scotland in the 1840s. Emigrants were drawn by the promise of a well-ordered Christian society and Scottish culture. Eighty per cent of the early emigrants were Scots.

However, Scots also liked the fact that the USA and Canada were more classless. One emigrant to Michigan, USA, wrote:

If you want to enjoy equality, social and intelligent neighbours with independence from browbeating superiors, I would say come here.

Conclusion

Some emigration was the result of poverty and unhappiness at the lack of opportunities in Scotland. The famine and clearances in the Highlands caused some of the worst examples of forced emigration in Scotland's history. At the same time, many Scots moved because of the chance of a better life elsewhere. It was the pull of opportunity that kept Scots emigrating for so long and in such big numbers.

Activity 1

Hot-seat game

Mindmap a list of the kinds of people who would have chosen to emigrate. After a class discussion, create a list of five characters who represent the main types of people who would have chosen to emigrate. Choose five classmates to act out the characters. Here is a list of possible characters:

▶ a young farm labourer
▶ a joiner
▶ a coal miner
▶ a landowner
▶ a doctor.

Those chosen to be in the hot seat should each draw up a short profile of their character. The profile should include a name, place of origin, education, family and at least three reasons for emigrating.

The others in the class should make up questions to find out who each character is and why they want to emigrate. Confirm the identity of the character being played and discuss interesting points and challenges to anything said by the hot-seat characters.

Question practice

Source A is from the 1906 annual report by the Quarrier children's home charity. It is about sending children to Canada.

SOURCE A

Much time has been taken up this month selecting and interviewing the lads we aim to send to Canada shortly. The children must be of the best, physically and mentally, and must pass a medical examination. Those who are now 'going west' know that work, which will provide an honest living, can be found by all who seek it.

Source B is by Annie Croall, who ran a children's home in Stirling. It is about the children she sent to Canada.

SOURCE B

In all the different departments of child rescue work, not one is more worthwhile than emigration. It is not only good for the country but best for the children. There is more scope for them in Canada. The boys and girls have every advantage on their side; they are strong and healthy.

1 Look at Source A. State the origin of the source. This means that you should identify when and where the source came from.
2 Compare the views on the children who emigrated to Canada in Sources A and B. This means that you should compare the similarities or differences between Source A and Source B.

Success criteria

▸ Include one factual point regarding the author, timing or purpose of the source.
▸ Examine the two sources in order to show two simple points or one developed point of similarity or difference.

Source C is about the reasons for emigration. It is written by a modern historian, Tom Devine.

SOURCE C

After 1860, Scots left their native land in search of more opportunity, 'independence' and through an ambition to 'get on' – hopes which could not be satisfied in Scotland itself. It is significant that the very poor were not usually among the emigrants in large numbers.

Source D is about the reasons for emigration. It is from an interview with Margaret Kirk, who emigrated from Scotland in 1923 after she had failed to become a doctor because of lack of money.

SOURCE D

There was loads of work while the [First World] war was on. As soon as the war finished, everybody was getting laid off. There was a depression in the country, and everybody wanted to come to America. There was nothing, there was no work, so they were gasping for a job. And America sent out signals that everything was wonderful here, so they came to America.

3 Use Sources C and D and your own knowledge to design a visual presentation explaining the main reasons why Scots decided to emigrate. This could be a poster, slide show, digital media product, video or any other appropriate format.

In your presentation you should:

▶ Explain in your own words what at least one of the sources tells us about why Scots decided to emigrate.
▶ Explain the main reasons why Scots decided to emigrate. You should talk about push and pull reasons.
▶ Give a brief conclusion in answer to the question: 'Why did Scots emigrate?'

Success criteria

▶ Explain at least one reason why Scots emigrated.
▶ Select relevant information from at least one of either Source C or Source D.
▶ Use your own knowledge (information not in Sources C or D) to give at least one reason why Scots emigrated.
▶ Provide a sentence giving an overall opinion on the question.

National 5

This task is intended to help you practise the 8-mark question in the external exam.

To what extent did Scots emigrate because of opportunities abroad, 1830–1939? (8 marks)

Your answer should include:

▶ An introduction which talks about the two main reasons why Scots emigrated: push and pull factors.
▶ A paragraph which discusses some evidence and reasons why Scots chose to move.
▶ A paragraph which discusses some evidence and reasons why Scots were forced to move.
▶ A conclusion which is based on the evidence presented and addresses the question.

Planning your answer:

▶ In small groups or pairs, mindmap the reasons why Scots emigrated.
▶ You might use your learning walls and fish-bone diagrams as a starting point.
▶ Group the reasons into push or pull paragraphs.
▶ Find connections between the different reasons and group them together. This will give you a structure for the order in which you talk about the reasons why Scots emigrated.
▶ Plan an overall response to the question.
▶ Show your plan to your teacher before starting your first draft.
▶ Read through your work carefully and mark any mistakes you spot with a green pen, then correct your work before handing it to your teacher.
▶ Rewrite the final draft of your answer.

Success criteria

Knowledge:

▶ Make a judgement about why Scots emigrated.
▶ Your answer must provide a balanced account of the different reasons why Scots emigrated and come to a reasoned conclusion based on the evidence presented.
▶ Up to 5 marks are given for the relevant points used to address the question.
▶ A mark will be given for each accurate point which is properly explained.
▶ You can get a further mark for each point by developing its detail or explanation.
▶ A maximum of 3 marks is allocated for relevant knowledge used to address the question where only one factor or only one side of the argument is presented.

Structure:

▶ Up to 3 marks can be given for presenting the answer in a structured way, leading to a reasoned conclusion that answers the question.
▶ 1 mark for the answer being presented in a structured way. The information should be organised and mention different factors.
▶ 1 mark for a valid judgement or overall conclusion.
▶ 1 mark for a reason being provided in support of the conclusion.

Experience of Scots abroad, 1830s–1939

Chapter 9 Where did Scots move to?

What is this chapter about?

Between the 1830s and 1930s, thousands of Scots left for a new life abroad. Altogether around 2.25 million people emigrated. Large numbers moved to England. Many Scots went further afield to North America, India, Australia and New Zealand.

By the end of this chapter you should be able to:

▶ Describe the impact of Scots in England.
▶ Describe the impact of Scots across the world.
▶ Explain the opportunities that were offered to Scots abroad.

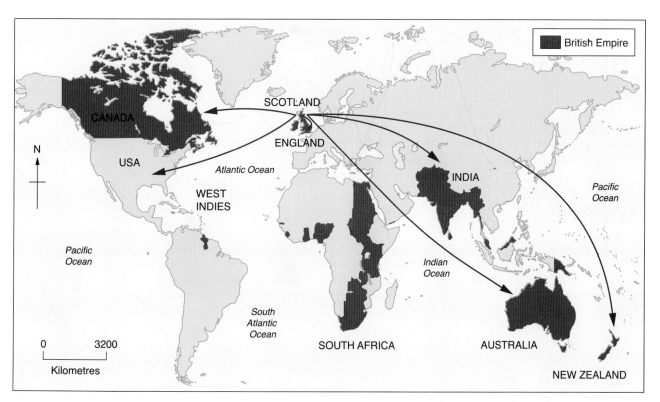

Countries where Scots moved to.

England

Between 1830 and the 1930s, around 750,000 Scots migrated to England. England was easy to get to and offered higher pay and opportunities for the enterprising Scot.

Some Scots only stayed for a short time. For example, the Scottish herring fleet would move around Britain. English fishing ports like Lowestoft and Great Yarmouth for a time had large numbers of Scottish fishermen and women fish gutters. However, most Scots stayed in one place; they were important as workers in English-based industries. From the 1870s, Scottish migrants to England were generally skilled. They worked in the coal mining and **heavy industries** that grew in the north and midlands of England. The textile, shipping and chemical industries of England were all influenced by Scottish workers. Scots also invested their **capital** in English businesses. England was also a popular destination for Scottish **graduates**, such as doctors. Aberdeen University found that between 1830 and 1882, of 1115 Scottish-born medical graduates, 298 spent all or part of their working careers in England.

> **GLOSSARY**
>
> **Heavy industries** coal mining, iron and steel making, shipbuilding and so on
>
> **Capital** something used to create wealth, usually money
>
> **Graduates** people who have completed courses or training resulting in an academic degree

Canada

Canada was a popular destination for Scottish emigration. The Scottish influence on Canada can be seen in the name of Nova Scotia, one of its provinces, which means New Scotland. Canada was attractive as it offered many opportunities in the fur trade and farming. It was also relatively easy to get to from Scotland. By the 1900s, steamships could make the journey in about a week. This meant that there were fewer delays in finding work and earning money.

United States of America

In 1931, there were 354,323 people living in the USA who had been born in Scotland. The USA was not part of the British Empire in 1830, but it had been in the past. In the late eighteenth century, the USA fought for its independence from Britain and won. However, a strong bond with Scotland existed. The USA offered a lot of opportunities for the skilled Scot. This was especially true in farming and business.

Australia

By 1900, there were about 250,000 Scots in Australia. The first Scottish settlers had been convicts who were sent to Australia as a punishment. Australia took a long time to travel to, but attracted emigrants because of its climate and opportunities in farming and business. In 1851, gold was found and this increased the number of emigrants from Scotland who were seeking their fortune. In the 1850s, around 90,000 Scots set off for Australia.

New Zealand

Many Scots settled in the South Island of New Zealand. New Zealand offered an attractive climate and was good for farming. By 1901, around 48,000 Scots lived in New Zealand.

India

India was part of the British Empire and was ruled directly from Britain after 1847. Many of the governors and government officials who ran India were Scottish. There were also many Scottish soldiers serving in India.

India was a popular place for Scottish traders to work in. Andrew Yule was one such man and the company he founded still exists and is now owned by the Indian government.

Activity 1

Mapping information

▶ Draw, copy or print a blank copy of a map of the world.
▶ Place this map on a much bigger sheet of paper. You will now have a large area of space around the edges of your map.
▶ Using the information in this chapter, label your map with notes about the impact of Scots across the world.
▶ Make sure that you leave space to add more information to your map.
▶ You could colour code the information by shading the countries/areas in different colours.

Activity 2

The challenge! How far can you go?

The following questions go up in level of difficulty in pairs. The first two are easy. The last two are hard. How many will you try to do?

1 Where did most Scots live when they moved abroad?
2 What sorts of jobs did Scots work in when they moved abroad?

3 Why did Scots choose to move away from Scotland?
4 Explain the impact of Scots on England.

5 How important were Scots in the development of the countries they went to?
6 'The most important impact of the Scots abroad was in medicine.' Do you agree or disagree with this statement? You will need to be able to support your answer with evidence.

Question practice

Source A is by a modern historian.

SOURCE A

Many Scots chose to leave the British Isles. Different destinations were popular at different times. Canada was the destination of choice for Scots in the 1840s and in the period leading up to the First World War. Australia and New Zealand were popular in the 1850s and 1860s because of the discovery of gold.

Describe where Scots settled when they emigrated. You should use Source A and your own knowledge.

Success criteria

Include at least two factual points or one developed piece of information on where Scots settled when they emigrated. These should be key points but may not be connected.

National 5

Source A is by a modern historian, Tom Devine, and is adapted from his book *To the Ends of the Earth: Scotland's Global Diaspora*, published in 2011.

SOURCE A

Scots have been leaving their homeland for centuries. Their movement to England has been a constant feature. Large numbers of Scots were attracted across the Atlantic and to India, Asia, South Africa, Australia and New Zealand. By Queen Victoria's reign, Scots could also be found in China, Japan, Argentina and other Latin American states; truly a global people.

Evaluate the usefulness of Source A as evidence of where Scots emigrated to from 1830 to the 1930s. You may want to comment on who wrote it, when they wrote it, why they wrote it and what they say or what has been missed out.
(6 marks)

Success criteria

- To get 1 mark, you need to explain the importance of each of the points you make
  To get 1 mark, you need to explain the importance of each of the points you make about the source.
- Up to 4 marks may be given for evaluative comments about origin and purpose. Comments about the origin may include an explanation about the type of source, the author or the timing of the source. Comments about purpose may include an explanation about why the source was written.
- Up to 2 marks may be given for your evaluation of the content of the source which you consider is useful in terms of the proposed question. For full marks to be given, each point needs to be discretely mentioned and its usefulness explained. If you list information, that will be considered to be one point and will get only 1 mark.
- Up to 2 marks may be given for evaluative comments relating to points of information not mentioned in the source.

Chapter 10 What was the contribution of individual Scots to the countries they moved to?

What is this chapter about?

Many Scottish emigrants made a huge contribution to their new countries. The reasons for this can be explained by the Scottish education system and the type of economy the Scots came from. However, not all Scots were successful abroad.

By the end of this chapter you should be able to:

▶ Describe the contribution of some Scots to their new countries.
▶ Explain why some Scots were successful in their new countries.
▶ Explain why some Scots returned to Scotland from their new countries.

Were Scottish migrants successful in England?

Many of the thousands of Scottish migrants who made the short trip to England did well. They prospered as farmers, engineers, businessmen and ship owners. Some were also successful as politicians.

Successful politicians

The first Labour Party prime minister was James Ramsay MacDonald. MacDonald was born in a two-roomed cottage in Lossiemouth in Moray. His mother was an unmarried servant girl. From these humble beginnings he rose to become prime minister in 1924 and again in 1929 and 1931.

Another successful Scot who did well in England was Katherine, Duchess of Atholl (1874–1960). She became the first female Scottish MP in 1923. She was a member of the Scottish Unionist (or Conservative) Party. She served as MP for Perth and West Kinross until 1938. In 1924 she became a minister in the Department of Education. She was the first woman to serve in a Conservative government and was also famous as a strong opponent of fascism.

> In what ways has the artist tried to show that Ramsay MacDonald was a serious politician?

James Ramsay MacDonald (1866–1937).

Successful inventors

Many of the important inventions that helped to make Britain a successful industrial nation in the nineteenth century were developed by Scots. James Nasmyth was one. Nasmyth was born in Edinburgh, but spent most of his working life in England. He is credited with the invention of the steam hammer. The force of this hammer could be varied so it could break an egg in a wine glass without breaking the glass, but could also shake buildings if it was used at full force. The Nasmyth steam hammer was very important in large-scale iron works.

John Logie Baird (1888–1946) lived for much of his life in England, although he was born in Helensburgh, Dunbartonshire. Baird was a successful engineer who is credited with developing the television. In 1926 he sent a television picture from one room to another. In 1927 he managed to send a picture between London and Glasgow.

The marine engineer David Napier (1790–1869) was another successful Scot. Napier's firm built the first boilers for steam-powered ships. He moved from Scotland and set up a successful business on the River Thames in London.

Nasmyth's steam hammer in action, as painted by Nasmyth himself.

Were Scots successful abroad?

The successful businessman

One Scottish emigrant was so successful abroad that he became one of the richest men in the world. That man was Andrew Carnegie (1835–1919). Carnegie was born into poverty in Dunfermline. His family emigrated from Scotland to the USA in 1848. Carnegie started his working life in a factory, and from there he went to work for the Pennsylvania Railroad Company. He worked hard and saved, building up enough capital to invest in business. Carnegie focused his energies on the growing steel industry and came to own a massive empire of efficient steel production. By the 1880s, Carnegie Steel was one of the largest producers of steel in the world. This business made Carnegie a very rich man. He sold his business in 1901 and devoted the rest of his life to being a **philanthropist**. He was particularly interested in furthering education and he gave money to found libraries. The first Carnegie library was opened in Dunfermline in 1883. Others opened in England, the USA, Canada, Fiji, the West Indies, Australia and New Zealand. Over 2500 libraries around the world were founded using his money. He also invested money in Scotland's universities in order to fund scientific research and to allow poor students to study. Yet more of his money supported music foundations. Cities like New York and Dunfermline have their Carnegie Halls, named after one of the richest men the world has seen.

> **GLOSSARY**
>
> **Philanthropist** someone who makes charitable donations of money intended to benefit others

Find or draw a version of this cartoon and label the parts of the drawing that show the following images: Scotland, USA, wealth and philanthropy.

Scottish conservationists and politicians abroad

John Muir (1838–1914) was born in Dunbar and is known today as the founder of the Conservation Movement. His family emigrated to the USA in 1849. Muir is famous for successfully campaigning for the preservation of wilderness areas in the USA. He was involved in setting up the Sierra Club, which helped to establish national parks across the USA. Perhaps the most famous wilderness Muir helped to preserve is Yosemite National Park. He wrote many books about his wanderings and the need to preserve the natural countryside.

Robert Underwood Johnson, who knew Muir, remembered him in the following way in 1916:

His countrymen owe him gratitude as the pioneer of our system of national parks. Before 1889 we had but one of any importance – the Yellowstone. Out of the fight which he led for the better care of the Yosemite by the State of California grew the demand for the extension of the system. His work was for the whole people, for he was the real father of the forest reservations of America.

A cartoon of Andrew Carnegie.

What does this stamp tell you about Muir's fame in the USA?

A US postage stamp showing John Muir.

71

John Alexander Macdonald and Andrew Fisher

John Alexander Macdonald (1815–91) was born in Glasgow and became the first prime minister of Canada. His family emigrated from Scotland to Canada in 1820. A number of Macdonald family members had previously emigrated so there was a family network when they arrived. Macdonald worked as a lawyer before entering politics as a Conservative, and became the first prime minister of the Dominion of Canada in 1867. Before his death in 1891, he had been prime minister for a total of 19 years. He is famous for helping to create the nation of Canada, its economic development and building strong ties with Britain.

Andrew Fisher (1862–1928) was born in Crosshouse, Ayrshire. Fisher was a coal miner and active in the trade union movement in Ayrshire. In 1885, he and his brother migrated to Queensland in Australia. When he arrived in Australia he continued to work in coal mines and play an active role in trade unionism. He was elected as a member of the Queensland Legislature for the Labour Party in 1893 and was prime minister of Australia three times between 1908 and 1915. He kept a distinct Scottish accent throughout his life.

Why were individual Scots successful abroad?

One important reason for the success of many Scots abroad has been recently discussed by historian Tom Devine:

Scotland grossly over-produced university-trained men in comparison to the rest of Britain. The Scottish educational philosophy, based as it was on 'useful learning', was admirably suited to the needs of the new lands for professionals and experts of every type.

Such an education system created skilled, practical workers. These workers also came from a developed industrial economy. Scottish workers were skilled at agricultural work and industrial work such as making ships, railway engines and steam engines. Important skills were developed and passed on through the apprentice system. In Scotland, workers were trained to be either engineers or farmers. These were useful skills for countries that were developing their own economies. Scottish emigrants were more likely than other emigrants to be skilled or semi-skilled **artisans**. Even Scottish prisoners, sent to Australia as a punishment, were able to read and write better than those from England and Ireland.

GLOSSARY
Artisans workers in a skilled trade

Language and religion also mattered. For example, in North America, speaking English gave the Scots a big advantage over immigrants from other European countries. The majority of Scottish emigrants were Protestant, which meant that they were not faced with anti-Catholic discrimination. Also, many Scots arrived abroad with money to invest. This was, again, popular in countries looking to develop their industries.

Were all Scots successful abroad?

Most studies show that about a third of Scottish emigrants returned to Scotland. Some were unhappy living abroad.

James Moreham arrived in Van Diemen's Land (modern-day Tasmania in Australia) in 1832 and quickly concluded that it was not for him:

What was said of this country I have found by sad experience to be false; I am very much dissatisfied with the place.

However, historians like Marjory Harper make the point that such returners were probably a minority. Many Scottish migrants went abroad with every intention of returning home. They went abroad to work, make some money and then return home. Money made abroad could then be invested at home. For example, the Forbes family in the north-east of Scotland used money made by family members in India to buy a country estate.

Many Scottish migrants who returned had jobs in which travelling abroad was necessary. Soldiers and missionaries are two examples.

Activity 1

Secrets of success

Take a whole page in your workbook or work file. Add the title 'Why were some Scots successful when they went abroad?'

Now draw up a table with two columns headed: 'Example of success' and 'Why successful?' Put the names of some of the successful Scottish migrants discussed in this chapter in the 'Example of success' column. Add at least two pieces of information from the textbook or your own research to explain why each of these people were successful. Be prepared to explain your answers.

As an additional task you could research other Scots who were successful abroad. Examples might include: George Simpson (1792–1860), Allan Pinkerton (1819–84), John Buncle (1822–89), Malcolm McEacharn (1852–1910) or Colin Campbell (1792–1863).

Activity 2

Wordsearch

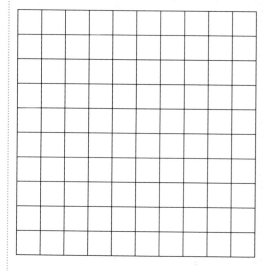

Make your own larger version of the wordbox shown here. Draw it large enough so that you can write words in the boxes.

Use the wordsearch grid to hide five main words (names or ideas) linked in some way with the contribution of individual Scots to the countries they moved to. Complete the grid with random letters to conceal your words. Do not show where the words are on your grid. Your partner must find them. So, write definitions of the words below or beside your wordsearch.

When you have completed your wordsearch puzzle, exchange it with your partner. Read their clues and find the words. As they solve your puzzle, you solve theirs.

Question practice

Success criteria

Knowledge:

▶ Make a judgement about the impact of the Scots on the countries that they emigrated to.

▶ Your answer must provide a balanced account of the ways in which Scots contributed to the countries they emigrated to and come to a reasoned conclusion based on the evidence presented.

▶ Up to 5 marks are given for relevant points used to address the question.

▶ 1 mark will be given for each accurate point which is properly explained.

▶ You can get 1 further mark for each point by developing its detail or explanation.

▶ A maximum of 3 marks is allocated for relevant knowledge used to address the question where only one factor or only one side of the argument is presented.

Structure:

Up to 3 marks can be given for presenting the answer in a structured way, leading to a reasoned conclusion that answers the question.

▶ 1 mark for the answer being presented in a structured way. The information should be organised and mention different factors.

▶ 1 mark for a valid judgement or overall conclusion.

▶ 1 mark for a reason being provided in support of the conclusion.

Chapter 11 What was the Scottish experience in North America?

What is this chapter about?

North America was one of the most popular places for Scots to emigrate to and they made an important impact as farmers, businessmen, engineers and politicians, and in education.

By the end of this chapter you should be able to:

▸ Describe the role of Scottish migrants in the development of the North American economy.
▸ Explain the importance of Scots in developing education in Canada.

Why emigrate from Scotland to North America?

North America includes both the USA and Canada. For most of this period, Canada was part of the British **Empire**, although it became a self-governing **dominion** in 1867. The USA had been part of the British Empire but had become independent after a war in the late eighteenth century.

Emigration from Scotland to North America had a long tradition and many Scots made the journey. The most popular times were the years up to the 1840s and from 1900 to the 1920s. The reasons for this have been explained earlier in this book, but historian Tom Devine has noted that:

> **GLOSSARY**
>
> **Empire** a group of states or countries under the control of another, usually overseas
>
> **Dominion** a part of an empire that was allowed to govern itself

No country could match the USA and Canada for ease of access, familiarity, economic opportunity, family links and availability of cheap land.

Scots were important in the development of the fur trade and the timber and agricultural industries in North America. People from Orkney and the Highlands dominated the fur trade through the Hudson's Bay Company and rival North West Company. Farming was the most common career for the majority of emigrants to Canada up to the 1860s. Even after this date, the Canadian government targeted Scotland as a place to find experienced farmers who could work on the vast lands of Canada's interior.

Scots were also employed in agriculture in the USA. They were skilled shepherds and could be found as ranch managers in US states such as New Mexico and Texas.

Most emigrants did well over the long term, but the work was hard. Michie Ewing emigrated from Aberdeenshire to Canada, and in 1857 he wrote home explaining:

I like the climate here and am fully convinced that many a poor man would be much better here than in Scotland. Yet there are many who come here who would be much better at home than here. Wages are high, but more work is expected, and unless a man be a good workman, few will employ him.

Some farmers became very wealthy. James Robertson, from the Strathmore area of Angus, wrote home in 1830 to say:

I bless God every day that I followed your advice not to farm at home and that I decided upon the United States as my place of rest.

Robertson lived in a large house and had staff to do much of his work.

Another example that shows the importance of Scottish money in the development of farming in the USA is that of the Matador Land & Cattle Co. In 1879, Hank Campbell, an American, persuaded four other investors to join him in setting up a ranch in Texas. In 1882, they sold the business to a group of Dundee businessmen for $1.25 million (the equivalent of over £130 million today). Many Dundee businessmen

had money to invest as they had made large profits in the jute industry. The USA was seen as a land of opportunity where more money could be made. Their investment in Matador was a good one. The company grew and eventually owned 40,000 cattle and over 600,000 hectares of land. The company was also managed by a Scot, Murdo Mackenzie. Mackenzie was born in 1850 in Tain, in Ross-shire. He was twice manager of Matador, once between 1891 and 1901 and once between 1922 and 1937.

Later emigrants were attracted by events like the discovery of gold in California in 1849.

> How can you tell that the company was successful?

The Matador Land & Cattle Co. headquarters.

Did Scots make an important contribution to the industrial development of North America?

Scottish emigrants were encouraged to relocate by better wages and conditions in jobs that they had always done. Some wages in the USA were three to four times higher than wages in Scotland. Most Scottish immigrants to the USA found work in the developing industrial economy.

Historian Tom Devine says:

Scots in the USA were to be found in skilled jobs in shipbuilding, construction, granite-working, engineering and mining.

By 1914, US industrial output was greater than Britain, France and Germany put together. Scottish people had made a contribution to this. The previous chapter described Andrew Carnegie and the US steel industry. Carnegie's factories produced cheap steel that helped the USA to build the railways and bridges that improved the economy. Steel was also important in that very American development: the skyscraper. Cheap steel was also important as it allowed the USA to compete against other industrial countries like Britain.

Andrew Carnegie's steel works in South Charleston, Virginia, USA, in about 1940.

What Scottish connection can you see in the poster?

Some economic developments were more important than others. One development that shows the contribution of Scots is the building of the Canadian Pacific Railway. This railway was important because it connected Canada's Atlantic coast on the east with the Pacific coast on the west. It allowed for the development and settlement of western Canada. A lot of the land in the west was prairie land. The Canadian Pacific Railway encouraged emigrants to Canada with cheap fares and cheap land to farm. This gave them a source of money which helped to develop Canada economically.

Political support for the railway came from the Scottish-born Prime Minister John Alexander Macdonald. Financial support for the railway came from the Scottish-born President of the Bank of Montreal, George Stephen. He had been born in Dufftown in Moray before moving to Canada in 1850. As president of the Bank of Montreal he helped to raise the $100 million needed to build the railway. The main surveyor and engineer for the route of the train was also Scottish. Sandford Fleming was born in Kirkcaldy in Fife and emigrated from Scotland to Canada in 1845.

A Canadian poster to encourage tourism.

The railway was completed in 1885 and helped to develop the Canadian economy. It also went some way to unifying the different provinces of Canada. Until the 1930s it was the only reliable way to travel across the vast country. It also encouraged tourism.

What was the Scottish role in developing education?

Scots also had a role in developing the education system in North America. Many important universities in Canada were founded by Scots. Examples include Dalhousie, McGill and Queen's universities. The kinds of subjects taught at these universities were also influenced by Scottish values. Courses were practical. In 1854, King's College in Fredericton offered the first degree in engineering available in Canada and the man behind its introduction was Scottish. Education was important because the people produced became the doctors, engineers and businessmen who developed the country.

Scots were important in developing farming, the fur trade, the banking industry, education and even government in both Canada and the USA. However, it is important to remember that other immigrant groups also played their part and were also influential.

Activity 1

A test of understanding

Work in pairs. Make up at least five questions that you would use to test someone's understanding of the experiences of Scots in North America.

First work out what you want to ask. You must have a clear idea of what answer you want for your question. Avoid questions that are vague and have no focus such as 'what do you think about the Scots in North America?' A good question would be 'what was the impact of Scots on American agriculture?'

Avoid asking questions that ask 'who was …' or 'when was …'. Also don't ask questions that have one-word answers – they are not allowed!

Your questions should be mature, well presented and test real understanding. The purpose is to help learning, not to catch people out with really tricky questions.

When you have both completed five questions, try them out on each other. Can your partner answer your question? And can you answer your partner's question in return? The ones to remember are the questions you could not answer. They show you what you are less sure about and are therefore a help to revision.

Repeat this exercise either now or at a later date – and try it out on different topics.

Activity 2

Summarise this chapter

A spider diagram can help you to summarise the information on the impact of Scots on North America. You might choose to do the planning for this task in pairs or small groups but it would be a good idea to complete the spider diagram on your own in your workbook or work file. This will give you a learning check on how well you know the information.

Using a large piece of paper, make notes on the topics listed here:

▶ fur trade
▶ farming
▶ steel industry
▶ railways
▶ politics
▶ education.

If you work in threes, one person can read, one person can listen and summarise, and one person can write down the information. Swap roles every time you change topic. Make sure you include at least two pieces of information about each topic.

Choose a double page in your workbook or work file and record the information you have researched in a colourful and well-presented spider diagram.

Question practice

National 4

Source A is about the importance of Scots in developing Canadian business and is from David S. MacMillan, *The Scot as Businessman*, published in 1976.

SOURCE A

*Scots gradually became some of the most important businessmen in the Fraser River Valley Gold Rush. Thomas and James Lowe were two of the first to come, arriving in 1861–2, becoming leaders of the business community. Scots also developed the timber trade. Gilbert M. Sproat was interested in shipbuilding and the **lumber** trade.*

Describe the impact of the Scots on North America. You should use Source A and your own knowledge.

Success criteria

Include at least two factual points of information or one piece of developed information describing the impact of the Scots on North America.

GLOSSARY

Lumber the raw wood cut from a tree in the timber business

National 5

Source A is about the impact of Scots on Canada, from William Wilfred Campbell, a Scottish–Canadian poet, in *The Scotsman in Canada*, published in 1911.

SOURCE A

In the making of this volume my chief object has been to produce a work which will be of use to those desiring knowledge of the origin of the Scottish settlement of Canada. When the Scot came to Canada he founded this country for Britain. It was he who discovered her wilds, named her rivers and her mountains. It was the Scot who gave a thorough and honest character to Canadian business and financial life. It must be a matter of pride to all men of Scottish descent in Canada to realise that the greater majority of our Governors have been of Scottish birth or extraction.

Evaluate the usefulness of Source A as evidence of the impact of Scots on North America. You may want to comment on who wrote it, when they wrote it, why they wrote it and what they say or what has been missed out. **(6 marks)**

Success criteria

▶ To get 1 mark, you need to explain the importance of each of the points you make about the source.
▶ Up to 4 marks may be given for evaluative comments about origin and purpose. Comments about the origin may include an explanation about the type of source, the author or the timing of the source. Comments about purpose may include an explanation about why the source was written.
▶ Up to 2 marks may be given for your evaluation of the content of the source which you consider is useful in terms of the proposed question. For full marks to be given, each point needs to be discretely mentioned and its usefulness explained. If you list information, that will be considered to be one point and will get only 1 mark.
▶ Up to 2 marks may be given for evaluative comments relating to points of information not mentioned in the source.

Chapter 12 What was the Scottish experience in Australia and New Zealand?

What is this chapter about?

Australia and New Zealand are a long way from Scotland. However, many Scots made this journey. The first Scottish emigrants to travel to Australia were convicts, but soon others made their way there. Australia and New Zealand were attractive places to go to because of their climate and developing economies. Scots played an important role in the development of these countries.

By the end of this chapter you should be able to:

▶ Describe what jobs Scottish immigrants did in Australia and New Zealand.
▶ Explain the impact of Scots on the education systems of Australia and New Zealand.

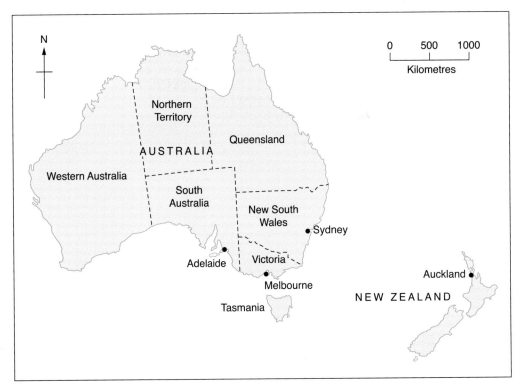

A map of Australia and New Zealand.

Were Scottish immigrants important in developing Australian and New Zealand farming?

Scottish emigrants were often good at farming and in **Australasia** this meant sheep farming. Historian Marjory Harper comments on the success of Scottish settlers:

*In the **Antipodes** the emphasis was on sheep farming. In return for small licence fees, many Scottish sheep farmers in Australia acquired huge acreages, flocks, bank balances and reputations.*

An Australian sheep station in 1902. Sheep were originally brought to Australia to feed the prisoners who had been sent there as a punishment. Both Australia and New Zealand were ideal for sheep farming.

One successful Scottish **pastoralist** was George Russell, originally from Fife. He farmed sheep in Tasmania, Australia, and died in 1888 leaving £318,000 in his will, which then was a fortune. John Macarthur was another important Scottish farmer who introduced **merino** sheep to Australia.

Many Scottish men who emigrated to New Zealand were employed as shepherds on sheep farms. These shepherds sometimes bought their own farms – one example is William Grant, originally from Ross-shire. Grant was hired as a shepherd and went on to become the owner of successful sheep farms.

Another reason for Scottish success in farming was the fact that Scottish companies had bought large areas of land in Australia and New Zealand. These companies often used fellow Scots to manage the land that they had bought. For example, the Aberdeen-based Scottish–Australian Company, formed in 1839, invested in farmland in Queensland and South Australia. Most of the managers employed by the company were Scottish born.

> ## GLOSSARY
>
> **Australasia** Australia, New Zealand and nearby islands
>
> **Antipodes** places on the other side of the world. In this case, Australia and New Zealand
>
> **Pastoralist** a sheep or cattle farmer
>
> **Merino** a breed of sheep that has soft and fine wool

Were Scottish immigrants important in developing Australian and New Zealand industry?

Scots were important in many Australian and New Zealand industries such as whaling, mining and engineering. Many Scots were attracted by the discovery of gold. The gold mines of New Zealand attracted many Shetlanders. Scottish miners were important in developing the coal and shale-oil mines of Australia. A good example of Scottish success in the mining industry is the story of James and Alexander Brown (1816–94 and 1827–77). They were originally from Lanarkshire and migrated to Sydney, Australia, in 1842. By 1868 they had developed a mining business that produced most of the coal in New South Wales, Australia.

Robert Campbell (1769–1846) is another important Scot who developed business in Australia. He was originally from Greenock. He was so important that he is known as the 'father of Australian business'. He developed a number of businesses including sheep farming and shipping. Another example is John Buncle (1822–89) who was a skilled engineer from Edinburgh. He arrived in Australia in 1852 and, as skilled workers were in demand, he found work easily. He eventually set up a very successful iron works in Melbourne.

Melbourne seems to have been a very 'Scottish' area of Australia. In 1839, one commentator said:

Melbourne is almost altogether a Scotch settlement, and the people are so far as I can judge altogether Scotch in their habits and manners.

Scots were also important in setting up and developing the Australian banking system. Banks like the Commercial Banking Company of Sydney and the Bank of Queensland were set up by Scots, and the Savings Bank of South Australia was managed by Dundee-born John Hector from 1848 to 1861. Banks were very important in lending money to help businesses to set up and grow.

A number of Scots were important in the shipping industry. In New Zealand, Henry McNicol, who emigrated from Greenock, set up a shipbuilding yard in Auckland. Shipping companies such as McIlwraith & McEacharn and Burns, Philip & Co. were set up by Scottish immigrants. McIlwraith & McEacharn shipping was the first firm to successfully freeze Australian meat and send it to Britain by ship. Scots were also involved in setting up the wine and brewing industries in Australia.

How can you tell that the owners of this company were proud of their Scottish heritage?

The flag of the McIlwraith & McEacharn shipping company.

Were Scottish immigrants important in Australian and New Zealand education?

Scottish education was practical in what it taught. A good education system helped produce **literate** and practical workers. This suited countries like Australia and New Zealand. The Presbyterian Church (or Kirk as it is also known), as well as some important individuals, was important in setting up this general and practical education system in Australia. The Presbyterian Church set up small schools across Australia. By 1850, there were 42 schools in New South Wales. Sydney University and Adelaide University also took Scottish education as their model. The Scottish education system of 1872 was also used as a model for New Zealand. The 1872 Education Act in Scotland allowed for free and compulsory education between the ages of five and 13. This was also introduced into New Zealand in 1877.

> **GLOSSARY**
> **Literate** able to read and write

It is important to note that not all emigrants from Scotland were successful in Australia and New Zealand. However, historian Tom Devine has noted:

Scots immigrants did leave a distinctive economic mark in the Empire, especially in Canada and New Zealand and, to a lesser extent, Australia.

Activity 1

Revolving circle

Choose either Australia or New Zealand to research, and write a paragraph of between 100 and 200 words explaining the impact of Scottish immigrants on your chosen country.

Divide your class into two groups and form each group into a circle. One group makes an inner circle and the other group makes an outer circle. You should face each other, standing opposite a classmate.

Take it in turns to exchange your information with each other for approximately one minute. Give your classmates a red, amber or green rating and at least one suggestion for information they might have included.

The inner circle then rotates clockwise and the outer circle rotates anti-clockwise. The new pair repeats the process.

The rotation continues until you all have had the opportunity to share information with at least two classmates.

Activity 2

Mapping information

Take a whole page in your workbook or work file. Either copy the outline of these maps into your workbook or work file or use a copy given to you by your teacher. Using this chapter, identify all the places mentioned and mark them on your map. Around and inside the outlines you have drawn, write down the industries and areas of life that Scots had an impact on in Australia and New Zealand. You now have a useful visual revision tool.

Question practice

National 4
Source A is about the impact of Scottish immigrants on Australia.

SOURCE A

Scottish immigrants had a big impact on Australia. Scottish farmers were very important in developing the agricultural industry of eastern Australia in particular. Scottish farmers were used to working in a harsh environment. Their investment in land brought large profits for some of the Scots who worked there.

1 Describe in your own words the impact of Scottish immigrants on Australia. You should use Source A and your own knowledge.

Success criteria
Include at least two factual points of information or one piece of developed information describing the impact of Scottish immigrants on Australia.

Source B is about the impact of the Scots on New Zealand. It is written by two historians, Jock Phillips and Terry Hearn.

SOURCE B

Scots made up about one in ten of the UK population. Yet from 1840 on, the Scots represented more than one in five of the UK immigrants to New Zealand. By 1891, about a quarter of the UK-born population of New Zealand was from Scotland.

2 State the origin of Source B. This means that you should identify who wrote the source and when the source was written.

Success criteria

▶ Include at least one factual point regarding the author, timing or purpose of the source.
▶ Explain your points fully.

National 5

1 Describe the impact of Scottish immigrants on Australia and New Zealand. **(5 marks)**

There will be not be a source in the exam to help you, but to get you started on your answer here are some hints:

▶ Scots made up approximately 15 per cent of immigrants to Australia.
▶ Scots made up approximately 25 per cent of immigrants to New Zealand.
▶ Scots were successful as farmers.
▶ Scots were successful in business.
▶ Scots influenced the education systems of Australia and New Zealand.
▶ Andrew Fisher was a Scottish emigrant who was prime minister of Australia three times.

Success criteria

▶ Include five factual points of information or at least three developed pieces of information on the impact of the Scots on Australia and New Zealand.
▶ Give accurate and detailed pieces of information that are properly explained.

Source A is about the impact of the Scots on Australia.

SOURCE A

A disproportionate number of Scots and Scottish Australians have been participants and leaders in Australian commerce and industry. In Melbourne, John Buncle was a foremost maker of agricultural implements. There were many successful flour millers: for example, Thomas Brunton and Mungo Scott in Victoria. There was also considerable Scottish involvement in metals, engineering, shipbuilding, textiles and building.

2 How fully does Source A show the impact of Scots on Australia? You should use Source A and your own knowledge. **(6 marks)**

Success criteria

▶ Place the source in context by explaining information in the source and applying that information to your own knowledge.
▶ A maximum of 2 marks may be given to answers in which no judgement has been made.
▶ Up to 3 marks can be gained for explaining points of information from the source.
▶ Up to 4 marks can be gained for explaining points of information from your own knowledge which are relevant to the question asked.
▶ Pieces of information from your own knowledge can be further explanation of points of information in the source or new points.

Chapter 13 What was the Scottish experience in India?

What is this chapter about?

Scots were important in how India was ruled and how it developed economically. Scots did not settle in India in great numbers. India is a good example of a place where people went for a short period of time then came home to Scotland. Other Scots made the journey to India then moved on to Australia and New Zealand. Some historians see India as a 'bridge' between Scotland and Australasia.

By the end of this chapter you should be able to:

▶ Describe the impact of Scottish traders, governors and soldiers on India.
▶ Explain the role of Scots in helping to develop education in India.

British involvement in India

Scottish and British influence in India started with trade. India during the period 1830–1939 covered modern-day India, Pakistan, Bangladesh and Sri Lanka. The East India Company was the main British company that traded with India. The company did not just trade, it also took control of Indian land. To begin with this was through bases or trading factories. The three bases were in Madras, Bombay and Calcutta. Rich parts of India, such as Bengal, were eventually controlled by the Company. British rule was not popular with everyone in India, particularly as the British tried to changed traditional Indian customs. In 1857, **sepoys** from the East India Company mutinied or fought for freedom, depending on your point of view. This led to a large-scale uprising against British rule in India. Eventually the **mutiny** was crushed by the British army. In 1858, the British started to rule India directly. This direct rule continued until Indian independence in 1947.

GLOSSARY

Sepoys Indian soldiers working for Britain

Mutiny where armed forces attempt to overthrow their commanders

Jute a long, soft, shiny vegetable fibre that can be spun into coarse, strong threads

The impact of Scottish traders on India

India was a common destination for the younger sons of Scotland's aristocracy and for young middle-class men. Many of these young men became traders. Scottish traders were to be found in the East India Company trading factories. Some Scots also became independent traders. An example of the kind of trade was when Glasgow merchants traded with the Bengal area of India and one result of this trade was the Paisley shawl.

The trade in **jute** is another story that shows the importance of India to Scotland. In the Scottish town of Dundee someone worked out how to make jute into a workable fibre. It was found that when treated with whale oil, the rough fibre of jute could be made pliable. Jute was used in the textile industry to make products such as sacking and sandbags. The raw jute was imported from Bengal in India where it grew. Eventually over 30,000 people were employed in Dundee's jute mills. However, it made sense to process the jute nearer to where it grew and so the trade also developed in India.

Nearly all the money to finance India's jute factories came from Scotland. In 1855, the first jute mill was opened by Scots at Serampore in India. By the First World War, Calcutta had 38 jute mills. These mills employed 184,000 workers and 1000 of these workers were Scottish.

The size of the jute mills in India can be seen here. This is the spinning department of one of the mills in Bengal.

Are the people in the photograph workers or managers? How can you tell?

Staff at a jute mill in India, 1910.

John Skinner is an example of how important the Scots were in India. In 1836 he helped to found the Bombay Chamber of Commerce. Skinner was also a member of the Bombay Steam Company, a business that shipped cotton between Scotland and India. He was also involved in the establishment of the Bank of Bombay in 1841. In the early 1800s, there were 14 Scottish merchant houses in Calcutta while the English had ten. Not bad considering that the Scottish people made up a tenth of the British population.

How important were Scots people as governors?

The East India Company was the face of British rule in India up to 1858. The most important company official was the Governor-General. Scotland had its fair share of Governors-General and **Viceroys**. Before 1830, there were Scottish officials such as Mountstuart Elphinstone. However, the most important and controversial figure was James Andrew Broun-Ramsay, Marquis of Dalhousie. He was born at Dalhousie House in Midlothian in 1812 and was Governor-General of India from 1848 to 1856. Broun-Ramsay is important because he expanded British rule in India. He developed a policy called the 'Doctrine of Lapse'. This meant that if an Indian ruler of an Indian state died without an heir, the East India Company could take over that state. Unsurprisingly, many Indian rulers did not like this. Some historians think this is one of the causes of the 1857 uprising against British rule.

Broun-Ramsay is also important because of his economic reforms. He encouraged industrialisation by developing Indian coal and iron. He also promoted railway building to help the British cotton industry. Broun-Ramsay oversaw the building of roads, bridges and canals and also large-scale **irrigation** works such as the 550 km Ganges canal. These irrigation projects helped to develop Indian agriculture.

> **GLOSSARY**
>
> **Viceroy** a ruler in a colony who governs on behalf of a colonial government
>
> **Irrigation** a method of watering crops and plants

How important were Scots as military leaders?

Many Scottish soldiers served in India and played an important role in leading the British army in 1857 during the Indian uprising. The most famous Scottish soldier was General Sir Colin Campbell. He planned carefully, fought hard and led British and loyal Indian soldiers to victory in 1858. Another important Scottish general was Sir James Hope Grant, who commanded the cavalry in the army.

Study the engraving. Do you think that Scottish soldiers were important in the retaking of Cawnpore? Give reasons for your answer.

The Highlanders retake Cawnpore in 1857. Cawnpore had been taken by the Indians, who rose up against the East India Company rule in India. It was recaptured by soldiers under the leadership of General Havelock.

How important were Scots in developing Indian education?

Some of the Scots who went to India did so as missionaries in the hope of spreading Christianity. One of the methods they used was to encourage education. Many missionaries thought that if people could read they would understand the Bible and see the word of the Christian God.

Many schools and universities in India were set up by these missionaries. Two good examples are the Reverend Alexander Duff, who helped to set up the University of Calcutta in 1857, and Dr John Wilson, who spent 47 years of his life working in Bombay.

Activity 1

Summarise this chapter

Take a whole page in your workbook or work file. Add the title 'The impact of Scots in India'.

Now draw up a table with four columns headed, 'Industry', 'Rulers', 'Soldiers' and 'Education'. In each column, list the names of key people, events and industries that relate to the Scots in India.

Now, write a short paragraph answering the following question: 'What was the most important effect Scots had in India?' You will have to support your answer with evidence from the table you have drawn up.

Activity 2

As a journalist you have been asked to investigate and report on the impact Scottish people made on India. Think about what sort of questions you might be looking for answers to. To help get you started, here are some hints:

▶ What jobs did Scots do in India?
▶ Were Scots successful when they came to India?
▶ Did the actions of some Scots cause problems in India?
▶ Why were some Scots so keen to educate Indians?

Write these questions down in your workbook or work file and then add at least one more to those provided. Find evidence to answer these questions and note your answers in your workbook or work file.

Now you can plan your article. Make notes and structure what you are going to write in your report. Write the first draft of your article.

Read through your work carefully and mark any mistakes you spot with a green pen, then correct your work before handing it to your teacher.

Ensure that information which answers all of the questions can be found in your article. Your article should be structured and well organised.

Question practice

National 4

Source A is about the role of Scots in India.

SOURCE A

The Marquis of Dalhousie made a greater impact on British India than any other Governor-General. He wanted to encourage the economic development of India. To do this he encouraged the growth of railways, and introduced the postage system and the electric telegraph.

1 Explain in your own words the impact of Scots on India. You should use Source A and your own knowledge.

Success criteria

Include at least one piece of information explaining the impact of Scots on India.

Sources B and C are about the relief of Cawnpore during the Indian mutiny.

SOURCE B

Cawnpore was recaptured from the mutineers by men of the 84th and 78th Highland regiments. Not a single British person was found to have survived. Every woman and child had been slaughtered in the Ladies' House. Brigadier-General James Neill issued an order that every captured rebel should be forced to clean a portion of the blood-stained house with his tongue before his execution.

SOURCE C

The dreadful punishment Neill came up with was to force the Indians into the blood stained room and force them to lick up some of the gore. He wanted to humiliate the prisoners before executing them. Cawnpore had been recaptured by Scottish regiments in July 1857 during the Indian mutiny. British soldiers were horrified by the butchery of the British residents of the town.

2 Compare the views in Sources B and C about the Indian mutiny. Describe in detail their similarities and/or differences. You can also briefly compare the overall attitude of the sources.

Success criteria

▸ Examine the two sources in order to show two simple points of comparison or make one developed point of similarity or difference.

▸ A simple comparison: 'Source B says … and Source C says … ' will get 1 mark.

▸ A developed comparison: 'Sources B and C agree about the role of the Highland regiments in recapturing Cawnpore. Source B says … and Source C says … ' will get 2 marks.

National 5

1 Describe the impact of Scots on India. **(5 marks)**

There will not be a source in the exam to help you, but to get you started on your answer here are some hints:

▶ impact as traders
▶ impact in developing India's economy
▶ impact as rulers in India
▶ impact as soldiers in India
▶ impact on developing India's education system.

Success criteria

▶ Include five factual points of information or at least three developed pieces of information on the impact of Scots on India.
▶ Give accurate and detailed pieces of information that are properly explained.

Source A is about the role of the James Andrew Broun-Ramsay, Marquis of Dalhousie in developing India.

SOURCE A

Dalhousie pursued a programme of intense Westernisation in British India. He created a department of public works in India. This set about giving India systems of railways, canals, posts and telegraphs that were better than those in most European countries. He launched industrialisation by developing resources of coal and iron, he improved agriculture by schemes of irrigation, with encouragement for the cultivation of tea and for forestry.

2 How fully does Source A explain the impact made by Scots on India? You should use Source A and your own knowledge. **(6 marks)**

Success criteria

▶ Place the source in context by explaining information in the source and applying that information to your own knowledge.
▶ A maximum of 2 marks may be given to answers in which no judgement has been made.
▶ Up to 3 marks can be gained for explaining points of information from the source.
▶ Up to 4 marks can be gained for explaining points of information from your own knowledge which are relevant to the question asked.
▶ Pieces of information from your own knowledge can be further explanation of points of information in the source or new points.

Chapter 14 Were Scots always wanted abroad?

What is this chapter about?

Emigrants from Scotland were not always welcomed in the countries they went to. When Scots arrived in places like the USA, Canada, India, Australia and New Zealand they came into contact with people who already lived there. In North America there were Native American tribes and Innuit peoples. In Australia there were the Aborigines and in New Zealand there were the Maoris. In India there were many different native peoples. Some Scottish settlers behaved badly towards the native people.

By the end of this chapter you should be able to:

▶ Describe the ways in which some Scottish settlers treated native people.
▶ Explain why native people were not happy with some of the people who arrived in their lands.

Native people

When the number of immigrants to countries was small, there were few problems with native people. However, as the number of immigrants grew, problems arose as native people saw these immigrants as a threat to their way of life.

Why did fighting take place between settlers and native people?

Immigrants began to destroy the traditional **nomadic** way of life that some of the native people had. Aborigines in Australia and Native Americans in the USA suffered from this. In the case of the USA, Native Americans had their lands taken and were forced to live in places called **reservations**.

Fighting would break out between the settlers and native people. The problem for the native people was that immigrants like the Scots had better weapons and were able to kill the native people who resisted.

> ### GLOSSARY
> **Nomadic** moving from place to place
> **Reservations** areas of land set aside for Native Americans by the US government

Australia

One Scottish settler in Australia explained why the Aborigines were not able to resist effectively:

Our natives have been much more quiet lately and I think every year they will become more accustomed to our ways. If not civilised, they now begin to find out that the power of our gunpowder is more deadly than their spears.

Scots were capable of very violent and brutal behaviour. One example is that of Major Donald Macleod. He emigrated to Australia in 1820 from Talisker, Isle of Skye.

Eventually he controlled over 80 square kilometres of land for sheep farming. This was only possible after the slaughter of the local Aboriginal people. Other events like the Warrigal massacre of 1843 also saw the killing of Aboriginal people in Australia by Scottish settlers.

An artist's view of relations between Aborigines and immigrants in Australia.

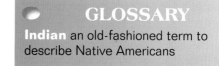

Who does the artist have sympathy with? How can you tell?

USA

Gavin Newhall from Kirkcudbrightshire arrived in Oregon in the USA in 1876 and wanted to be a farmer. The Native American tribes did not want to live on the reservations that they had been forced to move to. Newhall described what happened:

*They have broken out [of their reservation] and killed a good many whites and some soldiers. There are a good many volunteers besides a force of soldiers. The volunteers fight **Indian** fashion and kill every Indian they see, not like the soldiers who capture them and send them to be fed, clothed and pampered on the reservation.*

GLOSSARY

Indian an old-fashioned term to describe Native Americans

New Zealand

In New Zealand the relationship between local Maoris and white settlers was different from that in Australia. The Maoris of New Zealand signed the Treaty of Waitangi with the British government in the 1840s. This treaty gave the British the right to rule New Zealand, but the Maoris were to have their rights and land protected. Land could only be sold to the British government, which was then distributed to settlers. However, many Maoris were still very unhappy with the loss of their land to settlers.

Conflict broke out between the Maoris and settlers in a number of wars between 1845 and 1872. The Maoris proved to be tough warriors. A Scot, Sir Alexander Cameron, led the British soldiers who fought the Maoris. The eventual peace treaty that ended the wars was also negotiated by a Scot.

Did any Scots try to help the native peoples?

Many Scots did try to help the native people. Arthur Charles Hamilton Gordon was Governor of New Zealand between 1880 and 1882. He sided with the Maoris in land disputes and this got him into trouble with his own government. Other Scots fought hard for Aboriginal rights in Australia. Robert Christison tried to build good relations with the Aborigines. There is also evidence of intermarriage between Scottish and native people in places like Canada, Australia and New Zealand.

Activity 1

If this is the answer what is the question?

Below you will find a list of words or names. You have to make up a question that can only be answered by the words on the list. For example, if the word 'Aborigines' was the answer, a question could be 'What was the name of the native people who lived in Australia?' Write the question and answer into your workbook or work file.

- Maori
- nomadic
- reservations
- Warrigal massacre
- Treaty of Waitangi
- Sir Alexander Cameron
- Arthur Charles Hamilton Gordon.

Activity 2

The short challenge

Write a short summary of this chapter describing the main things that have happened. You must use *all* the words listed in Activity 1 in as few sentences as possible. Your title is: 'How did the Scots treat native people?'

Question practice

National 4

Source A is about the treatment of Aboriginal people by Scottish settlers. It is written by a modern historian, Malcolm Prentis.

SOURCE A

On the upper Yarra in Victoria, several early Scots settlers took pains to befriend the Aboriginal people. These included James Dawson, who was later appointed a Protector of Aborigines and published a book about them. The author Joseph Furby said that these pioneers' treatment of the blacks was excellent.

1 Why did the Scots treat native people in different ways?

Success criteria

- Describe at least one way in which Scots treated native people.
- Give at least one reason to explain why Scots treated native people in different ways.

Source B is about the treatment of the native people in the USA. It is from a letter by a Scottish settler, Gavin Newhall, to his mother back in Scotland in 1878.

SOURCE B

The devils had shot eight of my horses. I did not know how many others had run off. I travelled about 20 miles [32 km] with soldiers and volunteers until we met Indians. There were but 25 of us and the Indians were so strong that we turned off and rode through the mountains.

2 Use Sources A and B and your own knowledge to design a visual presentation describing the different ways Scots treated the native people they met.

Success criteria

- Describe at least one way in which Scots treated native people.
- Select relevant information from at least one of the sources.
- Use your own knowledge (information not in Source A or B) to give at least one reason why Scots treated native people in different ways.
- Provide a sentence giving an overall opinion on the question.

National 5

1 To what extent did Scots treat the native peoples of the Empire badly?
(8 marks)

To be successful in this task, your answer should include:

▶ A brief introduction which talks about the main ways Scots behaved towards the native people.
▶ A paragraph which discusses some evidence of Scots behaving badly towards native people.
▶ A paragraph which discusses some evidence of Scots behaving well towards native people.
▶ A conclusion which is based on the evidence presented and addresses the question.

Planning your answer:

▶ In small groups or pairs, mindmap the information on the behaviour of the Scots towards the native people they met.
▶ Group the information into 'Positive' and 'Negative' paragraphs.
▶ Find connections between the different pieces of information and group them together. This will give you a structure for the order in which you talk about the ways in which Scots behaved towards the native people they met.
▶ Plan an overall response to the question.
▶ Show your plan to your teacher before starting your first draft.
▶ Read through your work carefully and mark any mistakes you spot with a green pen, then correct your work before handing it to your teacher.
▶ Rewrite the final draft of your answer.

Success criteria

Knowledge:

▶ Make a judgement about the extent to which Scots behaved badly towards the native people they met.
▶ Your answer must provide a balanced account of the ways in which Scots behaved towards the native people they met and come to a reasoned conclusion based on the evidence presented.
▶ Up to 5 marks are given for relevant points used to address the question.
▶ 1 mark will be given for each accurate point which is properly explained.
▶ You can get 1 further mark for each point by developing its detail or explanation.
▶ A maximum of 3 marks is allocated for relevant knowledge used to address the question where only one factor or only one side of the argument is presented.

Structure:

Up to 3 marks can be given for presenting the answer in a structured way, leading to a reasoned conclusion that answers the question.

▶ 1 mark for the answer being presented in a structured way. The information should be organised and mention different factors.
▶ 1 mark for a valid judgement or overall conclusion.
▶ 1 mark for a reason being provided in support of the conclusion.

Source A is an extract about the Warrigal Creek massacre in Australia.

SOURCE A

The Highland Brigade, as they called themselves, sought out a particular band of Aborigines known to be difficult. They found them, more than 100 men, women and children, camped by a waterhole on the Warrigal Creek. The Scots galloped up, surrounded them, and then without warning began to shoot them down. The terrified people ran defensively hither and thither, some jumped into the water to try and hide under it. The Scots made great sport of picking them off as they had to come up for air. The creek ran red with their blood. The avengers, who paused only to cover up the bodies with sand from the banks, then cantered away in grim satisfaction.

2 How fully does Source A explain the relationship between Scots and the native people they met abroad? You should use Source A and your own knowledge. (6 marks)

Success criteria

▶ Place the source in context by explaining information in the source and applying that information to your own knowledge.
▶ A maximum of 2 marks may be given to answer in which no judgement has been made.
▶ Up to 3 marks can be gained for explaining points of information from the source.
▶ Up to 4 marks can be gained for explaining points of information from your own knowledge which are relevant to the question asked.
▶ Pieces of information from your own knowledge can be further explanation of points of information in the source or new points.

Glossary

A

Agricultural depression – a downturn in the money made from land and fishing from 1880 to 1914

Alcoholism – compulsive or addictive alcohol drinking

Anti-Semitism – hatred of Jews

Antipodes – places on the other side of the world. In this case, Australia and New Zealand

Artisans – workers in a skilled trade

Assimilated – people of different backgrounds becoming part of a larger national family

Australasia – Australia, New Zealand and nearby islands

B

British Empire – the network of land and countries controlled by Britain from 1830 to 1939

C

Capital – something used to create wealth, usually money

Census – a count of the population organised by the government every ten years

Clearances – the eviction and removal of a large number of Highland farmers

Cleared – a way of saying 'evicted' or 'removed' that doesn't sound so bad

Colonies – land or territories controlled by another country, usually a western European one

D

Depopulation – migration or emigration leading to a decrease in population

Dominion – a part of an empire that was allowed to govern itself

E

Empire – a group of states or countries under the control of another, usually overseas

F

Fenians – organisations that wanted Ireland to be independent from Britain

G

Graduates – people who have completed courses or training resulting in an academic degree

H

Heavy industries – coal mining, iron and steel making, shipbuilding and so on

I

Immigrant – a person coming to live permanently in a different country

Indian – an old-fashioned term to describe Native Americans

Industrial Revolution – a huge change in the economy where new methods are used to make things

Intermarriage – marriage between races or religions

Irrigation – a method of watering crops and plants

J

Jute – a long, soft, shiny vegetable fibre that can be spun into coarse, strong threads

L

Land factor – a landlord's agent who collects rent and deals with tenants

Literate – able to read and write

Lobby – to influence government officials to change a policy

Lumber – the raw wood cut from a tree in the timber business

M

Merino – a breed of sheep that has soft and fine wool

Migrants – people who travel from one place to another, often in search of work

Missionaries – members of religious groups who travel away from home in order to try and spread their faith's message more widely

Mutiny – where armed forces attempt to overthrow their commanders

N

Navvies – short for navigators; people who work as labourers on road or rail building, for example

Nomadic – moving from place to place

P

Parish – a small district, normally with its own church and a priest or church minister

Pastoralist – a sheep or cattle farmer

Peasant – someone who makes their living from farming a small piece of land

Philanthropist – someone who makes charitable donations of money intended to benefit others

Pogrom – an organised attack on Jews

Potato blight – an airborne fungus that causes potatoes to rot

Pull factor – an opportunity that encourages people to move abroad

Push factor – a reason that forces people to move abroad

R

Reservations – areas of land set aside for Native Americans by the US government

S

Sabbath – a day of rest and worship

Sectarian rivalries – divisions between two communities, usually over religion and ideas

Sepoys – Indian soldiers working for Britain

Smallholders – farmers renting a small area of land from a landlord

Stereotype – an image or set of characteristics that a lot of people believe represents a particular group of people

Strike – when workers stop working, usually to try to force an employer to pay higher wages

Synagogue – a Jewish house of prayer

T

Trade union – a workers' organisation that aims to protect members' pay and conditions

V

Viceroy – a ruler in a colony who governs on behalf of a colonial government

W

Weavers – people who make fabrics from fibres

Y

Yiddish – a language spoken by Jews

Index